Richard Owen

T0246503

Titles in the series Critical Lives present the work of leading cultural figures of the modern period. Each book explores the life of the artist, writer, philosopher or architect in question and relates it to their major works.

In the same series

Richard Owen

Patrick Armstrong

REAKTION BOOKS

For my brother, Tim

Published by Reaktion Books Ltd
Unit 32, Waterside
44–48, Wharf Road
London N1 7UX, UK

www.reaktionbooks.co.uk

First published 2023
Copyright © Patrick Armstrong 2023

Printed and bound in Great Britain by TJ Books Ltd, Padstow, Cornwall

A catalogue record for this book is available from the British Library

ISBN 978 1 78914 762 9

Contents

Henry William Pickersgill, *Sir Richard Owen*, *c*. 1845, oil on canvas.

Introduction

Sir Richard Owen, KCB, FRS, FGS, FRMS (1804–1892), was one of the ablest and most multi-talented British scientists of the high Victorian period. He was an all-rounder, a naturalist making major contributions to the study of both vertebrates and invertebrates: he was both a palaeontologist and a comparative anatomist, describing both the extinct organisms of the remote past and those still found around us in the world today. He was a great publicist for science and completely re-invented the concept of the museum, an associate of several members of the royal family and numerous distinguished churchmen, and received a dazzling array of the very highest scientific awards and honours. However, his relationships with his colleagues were often fraught.

He had numerous physical advantages, including that of being quite striking in appearance. He was over 1.8 metres tall (6 ft) and had an enormous, very prominent forehead. He possessed large and remarkably flexible hands, well-suited to their task of dissection. His contemporaries sometimes described him as a bit of a dandy.

He also had the enormous advantage of working at a time of rapid progress in British science: Charles Darwin (1809–1882), Alfred Russel Wallace (1823–1913), Joseph Hooker (1817–1911), Thomas Huxley (1825–1895), Charles Lyell (1797–1875), William Conybeare (1787–1857) and William Buckland (1784–1856) were all, to some degree, contemporaries of Owen – Buckland, at one stage, was a particularly close colleague. These 'men of science' all knew one another; frequently, several of them were in London at the same time, sometimes in the same room. Some of them are known to have conducted fieldwork when in each other's company. Moreover, the mid- to late nineteenth century was a time when the British imperial and naval powers were at their height. Hooker, Darwin and Huxley all made long voyages aboard Royal Naval vessels. Their ships, and countless others, brought specimens and observations back to Britain from throughout the empire and from elsewhere. Britain's imperial position also meant that there was a network of persons interested in science in many of the colonies, feeding information back into the scientific endeavours of their home country. Missionaries, administrators, medical men and army and naval officers corresponded with naturalists in their home country, to the enormous advantage of the latter. Owen, for example, built his career to a considerable extent on describing vertebrate specimens (fossil and contemporary) from Africa, Australia, New Zealand, Mauritius and the Americas.[1] Owen regarded it as entirely appropriate that colonial administrators, explorers and, indeed, colonial governors should provide him with a constant supply of material. Indeed, it was he who described some of the fossil mammals that Darwin collected while on his voyage on the *Beagle*.[2]

Although, at least at certain times in his life, he held ideas that might be considered to some extent vaguely evolutionary, over the decades before and after the publication of *On the Origin of Species*, Owen swung between being virulently opposed to Charles Darwin's theories and virtually claiming that he had himself thought of the idea of natural selection. Several times in his career, he was accused of plagiarism, claiming the work of other scientists as his own. While popular with at least some of his colleagues early in his career, he later attracted enormous controversy and resentment and was eventually shunned by many of those with whom he had worked on the councils of scientific societies and on government committees. To say that he was an 'interesting character' would be an understatement.

It is to Charles Robert Darwin, the originator (along with Alfred Russel Wallace) of the theory of evolution through natural selection, that Richard Owen is most often compared. There are striking similarities between the two men. They were both born in the first decade of the nineteenth century – indeed, only five years apart. Both were brought up in English provincial towns some distance from London: Darwin in Shrewsbury, the county town of Shropshire, close to the border with Wales; Owen in Lancaster, Lancashire, in northern England. Both were schooled close to their homes – Darwin at Shrewsbury School, Owen at Lancaster Grammar School – and neither of them particularly distinguished themselves as students. Both lost a parent very early in life: Owen's father died when he was only five, in 1809; Darwin's mother died in 1817, when he was eight. Owen, as a teenager, was apprenticed to a local apothecary and surgeon, while Darwin assisted his father, Robert Darwin (1766–1848), for a few months after leaving school. Both undertook medical training at Edinburgh University – indeed, they attended lectures by some of the same professors within a few years of each other. Both left Edinburgh before completing the course – Owen leaving after half a year, Darwin after two years. Both, to some extent, established their scientific credentials through major studies on marine invertebrates: Darwin's on barnacles, Owen's on the pearly nautilus.[3] There are similarities, too, in the vast array of honours that they were accorded in later life. Both, for example, were elected Fellows of the Royal Society at the young age of thirty, and both were awarded the Royal and Copley Medals of the Royal Society, along with the Wollaston Medal of the Geological Society during their later careers.

However, there were also significant differences. Darwin's family was considered gentry and, as a young man, Charles associated with members of the notable county families of Shropshire, while Owen's father was involved in trade. Darwin had a Cambridge education (Christ's College, 1828–31), and the advantages of considerable inherited family wealth, while Owen had always had to earn his living: this fact, in particular, irked Owen. While Owen sometimes seemed to positively court publicity and controversy, Darwin shunned it, adopting the posture of a retiring country gentleman, living at Down House in the village of Downe, Kent, for much of his life.

Perhaps it was at least partly these differences in background that eventually contributed to the enmity between the two men. Initially, they got on well together, the two colleagues co-operating over the descriptions of some of the fossil material that Darwin brought back from the *Beagle* voyage.

When Darwin was quite ill shortly after his marriage, Richard Owen was among the few of Darwin's scientific friends who visited him. In his *Autobiography* (written late in life), Darwin wrote that he 'often saw Owen, while living in London, and admired him greatly'. However, he continued: 'After the publication of the *On the Origin*, he became my bitter enemy . . . as far as I could judge, out of jealousy at its success.' Sometimes, in his earlier years, Darwin used to defend Owen to his friends, some of whom held a very bad opinion of him. The palaeontologist Hugh Falconer, whom Darwin thought was 'a charming man', described Owen as 'not only ambitious, very envious and arrogant, but untruthful and dishonest'. Looking back later in life, Darwin recalled that Falconer had said: 'You will find him out one day,' and so it proved;[4] following 'The Great Debate' on *On the Origin* in Oxford in 1860, Darwin noted in a letter to Falconer: 'I do heartily enjoy Owen having a good setting down – his arrogance and malignity are too bad.'[5]

The defenders of the Darwinian position, such as Thomas Huxley, a comparative anatomist, and Joseph Hooker, a botanist, similarly received their own servings of Owen's bile. In particular, Owen was intensely envious of Hooker's position as the director of the Royal Botanic Gardens, with its great herbarium at Kew, and believed that the Kew establishment should be subordinate to the British Museum (and thus to Owen); this was where, for the latter part of his career, Owen ruled supreme over the natural history collections. Owen tried hard to discredit Joseph Hooker; words such as 'spiteful', 'bitter', 'sneering', 'dishonest', 'hateful', 'malice', 'liar' and 'utter untrustworthiness' litter the opinions expressed in the private letters of his scientific contemporaries.

Some more recent opinions have been equally harsh: R. B. Freeman, in his authoritative work *Charles Darwin: A Companion*, published in 1978, put it as follows: 'Owen: the most distinguished vertebrate zoologist and palaeontologist . . . but a deceitful and odious man'. The same phrase was quoted by P. van Helvert and J. van Wyhe in their own book, *Darwin: A Companion*, in 2021. This last work quotes Mrs Carlyle as saying that 'Owen's sweetness reminded her of sugar of lead.'[6]

And yet, and yet . . . There are those who argue that the flaws in the personality of an individual are irrelevant when one is evaluating his or her contribution to science (or to art, literature or music). Such scholars would ignore Owen's quarrelsomeness and instead emphasize his contribution to the development of science in the nineteenth century, his enormous contribution to the basic understanding of the commonality seen in the structure of the vertebrates, and his establishment of palaeontology as a separate sub-discipline. In his defence, it has been pointed out that Richard Owen was a loving family man, a competent musician, a lover of opera, and one who read the works of Dickens (with whom he corresponded) and enjoyed the plays of Shakespeare.[7] In addition, not all those who had dealings with Richard Owen were as derogatory as some (but by no means all) of his scientific colleagues: Caroline Fox, a notable diarist and a member of a distinguished Quaker family, wrote after meeting him that he was 'very delightful', and commented: 'He is passionately fond of scenery: indeed, all that the Infinite Mind has impressed on matter has a charm and a voice for him.'[8]

As we shall see, there were plenty of Owen's contemporaries who gave him as good as they got. Thomas Huxley, oftentimes referred to as 'Darwin's Bulldog', was a particular antagonist, and was often quite savage in his dealings with Owen. Yet here, too, there were similarities: both Owen and Huxley sought to remove science from the realm of the dilettante and establish it as a worthwhile profession and, moreover, to establish their own positions within the scientific community.

Owen was indeed a complex individual. This book aims to explore some of the facts of the life and work of this enigmatic character and perhaps attempt to explain some aspects of his extraordinary personality.

1

Northern Origins: Childhood and Early life

Born on 20 July 1804, Richard Owen was the youngest of six siblings. His early circumstances were relatively humble, although not impoverished, and some of his ancestors had been prosperous landowners in Buckinghamshire. His father, also named Richard Owen (1754–1809), was a West Indian merchant who died when young Richard was just five years old. Some of Richard Sr's business enterprises in the West Indies had run into difficulties and he had incurred serious debts. His elder son, James Hawkins Owen, seems to have followed Richard Sr into the Caribbean region, for it is recorded that he died of yellow fever and was buried in Demerara, in what was then British Guiana (now Guyana), on 22 April 1827.

Richard Owen's mother (née Parrin, later Longworth) had been twice widowed: of Huguenot extraction, she too had a number of notable persons among her ancestors. On the death of her second husband, she opened a school for girls to help support her family.

Owen's early life and schooldays were spent in the town of Lancaster in northern England, and he entered Lancaster Grammar School (founded around 1235; after 1851, it was known as the Lancaster Royal Grammar School) at the age of six. The headmaster was the Reverend Joseph Rowley, MA, who was, apparently, Richard's godfather, and lived quite close by. Nevertheless, one of his teachers described the young Richard as being 'lazy and impudent' while at school.[1] Moreover, it is recorded that: 'At that time Owen did not apparently exhibit any marked fondness for study,' and he was 'exceedingly mischievous'. It is of interest that the young Richard Owen attended the school at the same time as

William Whewell (1794–1866), later famous as a great polymath, scientist, Anglican priest, philosopher, theologian, historian of science and, eventually, Master of Trinity College, Cambridge; at times, he was one of Owen's greatest supporters. However, Whewell was several years Owen's senior, although they seem to have been quite friendly in later life.

In August 1820, just after his sixteenth birthday, Richard Owen was apprenticed to a local surgeon and apothecary, Leonard Dickson. In his indenture, or deed of apprenticeship, it was agreed that he was to be taught the 'arts, businesses, professions and mysteries of a surgeon apothecary and man-midwife'. However, Dickson died two years later, and the apprenticeship was transferred to John Seed. A year later, Seed accepted a position as a surgeon in the Royal Navy. Affixed to Owen's indenture to Seed was a statement, written in Seed's own hand, declaring that 'Mr Owen's general conduct during the time he was with me has my highest commendation, and at all times I shall be happy to bear testimony to his most deserving merits, as well as to his respectability.' Following Seed's enlistment in the Navy, Owen's apprenticeship was again transferred, in September 1823, this time to James Stockdale Harrison.

For his initial apprenticeship to Dickson, Owen had the task of assisting him when he was the surgeon of Lancaster County Gaol, which was situated in Lancaster Castle, a forbidding medieval fortress – the building remained a prison until 2011. Owen used to tell tales of how the wind used to whistle, scream and howl around the stone towers and along the corridors on winter nights. It is thus unsurprising that when just a teenager sometimes required to attend the post-mortems held for those unfortunates who, as he put it later, 'by natural death are liberated from prison', his mind occasionally wandered into 'weird, ghostly imaginings'. Despite this, he greatly valued the instruction in anatomy that this training afforded, although some of his anecdotes associated with these days are macabre. For example, on one cold and frosty winter's night, Richard, no doubt strictly out of scientific curiosity, wished to secure the head of a man of 'Ethiopian race' who had died in the

Richard Parr, after William Westall, *Lancaster Castle*, 1830, engraving.

gaol, for the purposes of dissection. He severed the head, concealing it in a bag, and signified to the guard, as he left the prison, that the corpse was now ready for interment. Owen takes up the tale:

> As soon as I was outside I began to hurry down the hill; but the pavement was coated with a thin sheet of ice, my foot slipped, and . . . I lost my balance and fell forward with a shock that jerked the head out of the bag, and sent it bounding down the slippery surface of the steep descent. As soon as I recovered my legs, I raced desperately after it, but was too late to arrest its progress. I saw it bounce against the door of a cottage . . . which flew open and received me at the same time. I heard shrieks and saw the whisk of a garment of a female . . . the ghastly head was at my feet. I seized it and retreated, wrapping it in my cloak . . . I never stopped till I reached the surgery.[2]

Owen never completed his apprenticeship in Lancaster – possibly the frequent changes in the master to whom he was apprenticed were disruptive. In October 1824, he travelled to Edinburgh, a somewhat grey city that was, however, sometimes known as 'the Athens of the North', and enrolled at the university's medical school, which was then the leading institution for medical training in Britain. He seems to have studied hard, attending the lectures of Thomas Charles Hope on chemistry and pharmacy, those of James Home on the practice of medicine, John Mackintosh on midwifery and Andrew Duncan on *materia medica* (the name given to the body of knowledge regarding the materials used in healing, that is, medicines, the study of which is now usually referred to as pharmacology). He also attended the lectures given by Robert Jameson on natural history, as well as those of Alexander Monro (tertius) on anatomy. Unfortunately, Owen's time in Edinburgh was not a complete success. Duncan was in his eighties at the time, and, although some descriptions maintain that he remained active until he died in 1828, a certain spark must surely have already gone. Jameson, whose lectures on geology Darwin also attended and considered boring, was little better; nor was Monro, of whom Darwin opined that he 'made his lectures on human anatomy as dull as he was himself'. Owen's evaluation was similar: he is on record as stating that Monro lectured 'from the notes used by his grand-father and father, both of whom had successively occupied the chair of Anatomy before him . . . these lectures were found to be neither of

Thomas H. Shepherd, *The Canongate, Edinburgh*, 1831, engraving. Edinburgh was sometimes referred to as 'the Athens of the North'.

T. Hodgetts, after J.S.C. Syme, *John Barclay*, 1820, mezzotint.

particular interest, nor yet sufficiently up to date.'³ In light of the consistently rather poor teaching within the university, Richard Owen went to the external course given by John Barclay (1758–1826), who had studied medicine in Edinburgh and London; each year, he presented two complete courses of human anatomy, one in the morning, and one in the evening, for every winter session. He also gave courses on comparative anatomy. His classes had an excellent reputation, although they were strictly 'extra-mural', being given outside the university. Owen seems to have got on well with Barclay, and it seems possible that he absorbed something more than merely a knowledge of anatomy: a philosophical approach to science, a 'transcendentalism', an appreciation of the fact that pure, observational science does not always provide all the answers.[4] John Barclay gave Owen a good report at the end of the course that he took with him, along with his advice to transfer to St Bartholomew's Hospital in London. Perhaps he recognized Owen's ability, and knew only too well the imperfections of the official Edinburgh course. In any event, Barclay must have provided a laudatory reference to his London colleague and friend, for, in the early summer of 1825, Richard Owen introduced himself to John Abernethy, a surgeon and lecturer in surgery at St Bartholomew's Hospital, only some seven months after he had first journeyed to Edinburgh.

From the day he arrived at St Bartholomew's, Owen's future was assured. His early experiences in the north of England and Scotland had provided a firm foundation for his later life: a loving family home (he always wrote regularly to his mother and visited Lancaster whenever he could), an acquaintance with one who was to become a great Cambridge academic (William Whewell, who was later to provide encouragement and support), an excellent knowledge of anatomy, gained partly from watching post-mortems at Lancaster Gaol, and an obviously laudatory reference from Edinburgh's John Barclay. Young (twenty years old) and naive he may have been, but he already held several useful trump cards.

2

Early Days in London: St Bartholomew's Hospital, the Zoological Society and the Royal College of Surgeons

After Lancaster and Edinburgh, arriving in London was a shock. Owen later commented: 'When I arrived for the first time in London . . . I had not one single friend'; to begin with, the only link with his 'Northern friends' was the introduction letter from Barclay in Edinburgh to John Abernethy, who was initially somewhat abrupt. However, he offered the young medical student the post of prosector for his lectures in anatomy. The duties of a prosector included preparing and undertaking the preliminary dissection of the cadavers that were provided for lectures: 'The subjects provided for lectures were often sounder and in fresher condition, comparatively speaking, than was usually the case in those body-snatching days.'[1]

While working with Abernethy, Owen further improved his skills of dissection, which were probably already good; indeed, he read a couple of his papers before the St Bartholomew's Medical and Philosophical Society. Somehow, at Lancaster Gaol, in his much-disrupted apprenticeship, and in the short time he had spent in Edinburgh, plus a few months at St Bartholomew's, he had learned enough to obtain his membership of the Royal College of Surgeons, on 18 August 1826, his diploma being signed by Abernethy and nine other distinguished surgeons (Abernethy's connections were, thus, proving invaluable), a little over a year after he had moved south from Edinburgh. He set up a medical practitioner's in Carey Street, Lincoln's Inn Fields, in the heart of London's legal quarter, and built up a small practice among the lawyers.

In 1799 the British government purchased the collection of the pioneer surgeon John Hunter (1728–1793), which was, in due course, presented to the Royal College of Surgeons. This formed the basis of the Hunterian Collection, which at that time was curated by William Clift (1775–1849), who had been responsible for the collections for many years, almost since Hunter's time. As well as dissected surgical specimens, the collection contained a wide variety of animal specimens preserved in alcohol, some of them dating from 'the circumnavigatory voyage of Captain Cook'; these had been presented to John Hunter by Sir Joseph Banks, the botanist who had accompanied Cook on this voyage from 1768 to 1771. In 1826 Abernethy was the President of the Royal College of Surgeons, and so had a special responsibility for the collection; he was concerned that it had been neglected for years – Clift had received his training in art, not in medicine or science – and he thought that Owen was the ideal person to undertake its organization. Owen had probably absorbed some of John Barclay's ideas on comparative anatomy; by then, he had accrued a superb level of knowledge of human anatomy, in addition to his great skill in dissection. Accordingly, he was appointed as the assistant conservator, at a salary of £120 per annum, which was later increased to £150, and then to £200.

Richard Owen's immediate task was to identify and label the collection, comprising over 13,000 specimens, and prepare a catalogue: much of the documentation associated with the collection had been lost or destroyed. This task took Owen several years but provided him with experience and training in comparative anatomy that he could probably not have gained in any other way. The back story to this loss of documentation was that Everard Home (1756–1832), the brother-in-law of John Hunter and an eminent surgeon in his own right, had had custody of some of the documents, and is reported to have plagiarized them in some of his publications. Sources differ as to whether he deliberately destroyed some of these sources to 'cover his tracks' or whether they were accidentally destroyed in a fire.

Meanwhile, Richard Owen had maintained his links with St Bartholomew's Hospital, where, in 1828, he was appointed to the position of lecturer in comparative anatomy. The salary for

Thomas H. Shepherd, *St Bartholomew's Hospital, London*, 1831, engraving.

John Abernethy, early 19th-century print, unknown artist.

this appointment was modest; even when combined with his remuneration from the Hunterian Museum (where his position was insecure, being held 'during the pleasure of the Board of Curators'), it was judged insufficient for him to get married. Since, by Christmas 1827, Owen had become engaged to Caroline Clift, the daughter of his superior at the Hunterian Collection, his position was rather difficult. The position of Conservator of the Collection had been promised to William Clift's son on his father's death or retirement; therefore, Owen felt he had to look elsewhere for advancement, so he applied for a post at Birmingham Hospital in early 1830. However, when he was interviewed, it became clear that the position was not all that it had earlier appeared to be, and he returned to London.

Although from about this point forward Richard Owen's focus shifted increasingly towards zoology, comparative anatomy and palaeontology rather than towards medicine and surgery, he did not entirely abandon medicine. In 1835, he published a paper on a microscopic parasitic nematode that inhabited the muscles of humans, *Trichina* (*Trichinella*) *spiralis*, the organism responsible for the disease of trichinosis.[2]

Thomas H. Shepherd, *The Royal College of Surgeons, Lincoln's Inn Fields, London*, 1828, engraving.

William Sharp, after Sir Joshua Reynolds, *John Hunter*, 1788, engraving.

By this time Owen was as familiar with the use of the microscope as he was with the dissecting knife. By early 1834, his lectureship at St Bartholomew's had been upgraded to a professorship. Sir Anthony Carlisle, the distinguished surgeon, who had in fact studied under John Hunter and had kept an eye on the young Richard Owen, was very discouraging. Sir Anthony wrote him a stern letter of disapproval – he was concerned that Owen's energies might be dissipated too widely. Sir Anthony told him that his first loyalty should be to the College of Surgeons and John Hunter's legacy, 'and few [medical] students will have the time and still fewer the desire to study philosophical anatomy'. However, as Owen's grandson and biographer commented: 'Owen's energy and powers proved to be such that no amount of extra work was permitted to interfere with his ordinary routine.'

Meanwhile, other opportunities were opening up for Owen. He became a life member of the Zoological Society of London in 1830 and was soon elected to the Council. This appointment gave him unfettered access to the Zoological Gardens, and he was able to dissect any animals that died in the 'Zoo'. It has been reported that on one occasion, his wife Caroline arrived home to find a dead rhinoceros in her hallway. It had been Owen who urged the Society to purchase the animal in 1834, and it was he who dissected it fifteen years later. A lengthy paper with a series of extremely detailed illustrations was published in the Society's journal in 1851, after having been 'read to the Society' in November 1850. The post-mortem performed by Owen led to the very first discovery of the parathyroid glands. It was not until decades after Owen's death that his contribution to the identification of parathyroid glands, now known to be of great importance to the endocrine system, was fully appreciated.

There were also 'some distant overtures' made by the Zoological Society 'to doctor their brutes'. Owen viewed the prospect of 'turning veterinary' with 'some degree of repugnance', and very little was heard of the idea afterwards.

However, the link with the Zoological Society also gave him an *entrée* to the *Transactions and Proceedings* of the Society as a venue for the publication of his research. His first significant paper was, interestingly (in view of his later disputes about the relationships between the great apes and humans), titled 'On the Anatomy of the Orang Outang' (1831). Among the creatures on which he wrote papers over the next couple of years, based on his Zoological Society dissections, were the beaver, 'Thibet bear', gannet, seal, armadillo, kangaroo, toucan, platypus and flamingo. A cheetah, crocodile, giraffe and dugong followed, and so it continued for decades: sometimes, the bulk of any particular issue of the Society's journal was written by Owen. The massive task of cataloguing the Hunterian Collection at the College of Surgeons, meanwhile, continued apace.

The young Owen was obviously a prodigious worker, as well as extremely able. In the years between 1830 and 1835, he wrote more than sixty scientific papers, quite apart from his work on the multi-volume Hunterian catalogues. He had the advantage that he was uniquely placed: he held a (part-time) lectureship at St Bartholomew's Hospital, had the Zoological Society's resources at his disposal and the enormous Hunterian Collection of the College of Surgeons at hand. Perhaps even more importantly, he had access to the governing bodies of these institutions, peopled as they were by men of the highest distinction and influence – some of them being members of the aristocracy. For example, at the time when Owen was proposed for membership of the Council of the Zoological Society, so too were 'two lords and a baronet': he would always rather enjoy being associated with the great, the good and the titled.

His network soon extended even further. In 1830, Baron George Cuvier, otherwise known as the distinguished French naturalist and anatomist Jean Léopold Nicolas Frédéric Cuvier (1769–1832), often referred to as 'the founding father of palaeontology', visited London, apparently to collect material for his 'great work on fishes'. Owen recalled:

> I made Cuvier's personal acquaintance at the Museum of the College of Surgeons and was specially deputed to show and explain to him such specimens as he wished to examine. There was no special merit in my being thus deputed, the fact being that I was the only person available who could speak French, and who at the same time had some knowledge of the specimens. Cuvier kindly invited me to visit the Jardin des Plantes in the following year.[3]

Baron Cuvier, to whom Owen did pay a return visit in July, August and September 1831, was extremely welcoming: Owen's grandson later wrote that 'he attended, pretty regularly, Cuvier's soirées, held on Saturday evenings, and enjoyed the music. [His diary and] his letters both devote page after page to the sights and amusements of Paris.'[4] These letters seldom mention the vast fossil vertebrate collection, although while in Paris, Owen did find time to receive some lessons on the cello. Nevertheless, it was here that he met the great German geographer and explorer Alexander von Humboldt, the French naturalist Étienne Geoffroy Saint-Hilaire and

C. Lorichon, after N. Jacques, *Baron Cuvier*, 1826, engraving.

several other leading French scientists. In spite of the recreational, rather than academic, nature of some of his time in Paris, Richard Owen does seem to have absorbed something of Cuvier's approach and expertise, as well as his 'transcendental' understanding of the natural world.

Cuvier's work is often considered the foundation of the study of vertebrate palaeontology. He expanded Linnaeus' system of classification to include both fossil and living creatures, and also established extinction as a fact: in his *Essay on the Theory of the Earth* (1813), Cuvier suggested that now-extinct species had been wiped out by intermittent catastrophic flooding events. Thus he became an influential proponent of the doctrine of catastrophism in geology – the idea that the Earth's history is to be understood in terms of long periods of stability, interrupted by occasional, sudden, catastrophic events, which he termed 'deluges'. His study of the strata of the Paris basin, written with Alexandre Brongniart (1770–1847), established the basic principles of what came to be known as biostratigraphy: the idea that there exist many layers of rock, each of which contains fossils belonging to a distinctive set of created beings and that each represents a particular time period or epoch. A catastrophe brought an end to each epoch in the world's history, causing the elimination of its current creatures, and a new geological period, with a new assemblage of created organisms, to begin. Cuvier was therefore strongly opposed to the notions of evolution that had been proposed by his countrymen Jean-Baptiste de Lamarck and Étienne Geoffroy Saint-Hilaire. Cuvier believed that there was no evidence to support evolution, but rather proof for the repeated cycles of creation and destruction of life forms by major extinction events.

Cuvier named the fossilized flying reptile, the pterosaur, *Pterodactylus*, and described (although he did not discover or name) the Cretaceous aquatic reptile *Mosasaurus*; he was also among the first to suggest that the Earth had once been dominated by reptiles rather than mammals. His position in European science was almost unassailable. In the year in which Owen and Cuvier met in Paris, the French novelist Honoré de Balzac heaped praise on his countryman. In Balzac's estimation, Cuvier ranked as the successor to Lord Byron, the great Romantic poet of that era. One of Balzac's characters wondered:

> Is not Cuvier the great poet of our era? Byron has given admirable expression to certain moral conflicts, but our immortal naturalist has reconstructed past worlds from a few bleached bones; has rebuilt cities . . . with monsters' teeth; has animated forests with all the secrets of zoology, gleaned from a piece of coal; has discovered a giant population from the footprints of a mammoth. These forms stand erect, grow large, and fill regions commensurate with their giant size.[5]

Despite the salons, the soirées, the cello lessons and the time spent seeing the sights, Richard Owen seems to have absorbed a substantial part of Cuvier's philosophy and applied some, but by no means all of it, in his later life and work.

Nevertheless, when he was referred to as 'the English Cuvier', as sometimes happened, Richard Owen was always quick to respond that he had ploughed his own furrow – he was 'the English Owen'. However, he did occasionally acknowledge his debt to the French pioneer. Indeed, he did this remarkably soon after meeting him in Paris. In mid-1832, the College of Surgeons sponsored the publication of Richard Owen's extremely detailed monograph *Memoir of the Pearly Nautilus, with Illustrations of Its External Form and Internal Structure*. It was 'published by direction of the College' – somewhat surprisingly, as it had little to no medical relevance. This painstakingly detailed work was about seventy pages in length and had eight finely drawn plates, showing the structure of this strange organism – a cephalopod that is related to the squids and octopi, but possesses a chambered shell, the individual compartments of which can be filled with or emptied of water, affecting the buoyancy of the creature. The first paragraph commences:

> The true relations of every class of animals are now acknowledged to depend on anatomical investigation: and

the necessity of this mode of inquiry has been rendered more especially obvious with respect to those tribes whose outward forms, being unsupported by any firm and resistant framework, present in consequence variations extremely disproportionate to the differences exhibited in habits and powers of action. In this division of animals, the most important and unexpected results have been obtained from dissection of the Cephalopods, which under a form approaching to that of a Polype, disguise an organization as rich in the variety of parts as it is peculiar in their mode of arrangement. Hence, they have afforded one of the strongest arguments *against* the theory of the single and unbroken series, for a long time supposed to be the natural distribution of the animal kingdom: and they have subsequently been deemed no less adverse to a more modern doctrine, which according to the consideration of the analogies, presented in the materials of individual organisms, seeks to reduce their varied plans of composition to a principle of unity. (Emphasis added)

Written, as it was, when Owen, 'a young man in a hurry', was around 28 years old, this could be seen as something of a 'declaration of independence'. He asserts that 'anatomical investigation' – careful dissection – was the only manner in which organisms should be investigated and their taxonomic affinities determined: this applied to invertebrate forms without any 'firm and resistant framework', as well as to vertebrates. Owen seems to claim, although his style is rather opaque, that his study of the pearly nautilus (*Nautilus pompilius*, a creature with a chambered shell found in tropical seas, especially near reefs and on the seabed off of the coasts of Australia, Japan and the Pacific islands) provides no evidence for the theory of the 'single and unbroken series' of organisms, and is instead in favour of 'the principle of unity'. This could be construed as his opposition to evolutionary views, such as those of Lamarck or Erasmus Darwin. He reiterated this point on page two of the same monograph, quoting Cuvier; writing of the Cephalopoda in general, he comments that 'they form not the passage to any other group . . . they have not resulted from the development of any other animals,

Cross-section of a Nautilus shell showing its pearly chambers.

and . . . their own development has produced nothing superior to them.' There is, Owen argues, a single basic underlying pattern to the structure of organisms. This is an idea to which he returned at a later date.

From around the time of the publication of the Nautilus monograph, which was translated into French and German soon afterwards, things seemed to go rather well for Richard Owen. He sent an advance copy to Professor Buckland and to one or two other important 'scientific men', to keep his name fresh in their minds.[6] Buckland's appreciation was important, as his support gave Owen an entrée into a circle of Oxbridge-educated collectors and naturalists, who were to become important to him. Typical of this circle was William Willoughby, who later became the Earl of Enniskillen.

In short, his publication on the nautilus was extremely well received, and he was proposed for election to the Council of the Zoological Society.

T. H. Maguire, after Antoine Claudet, *William Buckland*, 1849, lithograph.

Meanwhile, Owen had been courting Caroline, the daughter of his employer at the Hunterian Collection, and the two were wondering when they would have sufficient resources to get married. The possibility of a professorship of comparative anatomy at the College of Surgeons, with a salary of £500 a year, was discussed; 'a more regular and extended course of lectures' than had hitherto been the custom began to be mentioned.

Then, in September 1832, 'an event took place which entirely altered Owen's prospects at the College of Surgeons.' Until that time, Richard Owen was an assistant conservator, holding his post 'during the pleasure of the Board'. His fellow assistant was William Home Clift, who had been promised the position of senior conservator upon the death of his father, William Clift Sr; Owen had always assumed that there would be no possibility of advancement at the college.

On 11 September 1832 the younger Clift was returning home by cab, and as the driver turned a corner sharply, the carriage was overturned and young William was 'pitched on his head'. He was taken to St Bartholomew's Hospital, where he was attended by Owen; Clift had a fracture at the base of the skull and died a few days later. Shortly after this event, Richard Owen assumed the position of sole assistant in the Hunterian Collection, at the rate of £200 per annum, which was increased to £300 the following year. From another man's misfortune came considerable advancement for Owen.

Owen's success continued. In April 1833 he was elected to the prestigious St Bartholomew's Club and early in 1834 he was appointed to the newly established Chair of Comparative Anatomy at St Bartholomew's Hospital: he was confident that he could complete the duties of this post as well as those he had at the Royal College of Surgeons. Later in the same year, Owen was elected as a fellow of the Royal Society, his certificate being signed by the pioneer psychologist and surgeon Sir Benjamin Brodie, John Edward Gray, a zoologist at the British Museum, and polar explorer James Clark Ross, as well as a galaxy of other distinguished men of science and medicine. He was formally admitted to the Royal Society on 15 January 1835.

Following these varied successes, Owen felt able to take the plunge into matrimony, and on the morning of 20 July 1835 (his birthday), he and Caroline Clift were married very quietly at the church of St Pancras, Euston Square, after which they travelled to Oxford.

Caroline proved to be a worthy spouse. Not only was she an excellent wife and mother, but she was an able assistant in Richard's work: for example, she recorded in her diary that she sketched a wombat's brain and shark's teeth. She assisted in marking the proofs of some of his publications and was able to translate German scientific papers into English. Sometimes he tried out his lectures on her; on at least one occasion, she made it clear that a talk was 'too long'.[7]

Interestingly, in addition to his work on the Hunterian Collection and at St Bartholomew's Hospital, a productive scientific publication output and possibly some private medical practice, Richard Owen 'founded and wrote the greater part' of the *Zoological Magazine; or, Journal of Natural History*, this 'being a series of miscellaneous articles . . . on interesting subjects in Zoology, &c'. The journal was intended to be strictly popular, with articles on 'The Giraffe', 'The Elephant' and 'The Rhinoceros': there were striking illustrations of some of these beasts, a short piece on a tiger attack and some notes on the Canadian fur trade. 'Serpents' and electric eels also appeared on its pages. Spectacular facts and interesting snippets of information were the rule, rather than the employment of full scientific rigour. Owen was not afraid to appeal to the common man, perhaps hoping to increase his profile, or perhaps he saw the venture as having money-making possibilities – after all, at this point, he was saving up to get married. Only six issues of this monthly periodical appeared, published in the first half of 1833. Perhaps the workload was too high, or perhaps it was not as financially rewarding as Owen had hoped. Possibly the hierarchy of the College of Surgeons disapproved of this vulgar descent into the marketplace.

Just under a year after his marriage, on 30 April 1836, he finally achieved his longed-for election as the Hunterian Professor of the Royal College of Surgeons. It could be said that in many ways, Owen never looked back from that time onwards.

However, the scientific and medical circles of London were restricted, and so Owen seldom lost an opportunity to extend his influence. He frequently attended the annual meetings of the British Association for the Advancement of Science. In August 1838 he travelled to Newcastle-upon-Tyne in northern England, on board a ship from London. He always liked to be 'within the bosom of

Richard Evans, *Harriet Martineau*, 1834, oil on canvas.

the Church', and he wrote to his wife from Gateshead Rectory, just outside the town (Newcastle did not become a city until 1882): 'The *Ocean* arrived with her cargo of philosophy, and I ought to add, literature, for Harriet Martineau was on board. See other side.' On the 'other side' was a sketch of Harriet holding a huge ear trumpet.

It is interesting to reflect on the fact that Richard Owen shared a sea voyage with the pioneer feminist author and to wonder what they discussed. However, she was indeed profoundly deaf.

The meeting of the British Association for the Advancement of Science seems to have been extremely successful. Owen gave an extempore talk on marsupials that was about ninety minutes in length and managed to be elected as the secretary of a committee. He enjoyed an audience and took advantage of any opportunity for networking. By this point, the 34-year-old Owen was well on his way.

3

Monsters and Curiosities: Extant, Extinct and Non-Existent

Tales of enormous sea creatures, illustrations of dinosaurs, rumours of giant birds that were several times the height of a man – stories of the gigantic, the terrifying, the exotic and the dangerous have always fascinated the curious mind. Throughout his career, Richard Owen aimed to be accessible and, wherever appropriate, to appeal to the interest of the common man. He wrote numerous articles on popular science and gave many series of lectures that were open to the general public. He believed passionately in the value of museums for the spreading of knowledge.

Often Owen wrote scientific papers on creatures that would capture the public imagination. His first major publication was on the strange, beautiful and exotic pearly nautilus. In his continuing search for the novel and the grotesque, he was, to some extent, helped by his links with the Zoological Society and London Zoo; from a fairly early stage in his career, he had the right to study and dissect deceased animals from the zoo. As Owen's influence and reputation spread, he was sometimes offered animals from other sources. In the first few years of his career (1830–34), Owen had written papers on the anatomy of a great variety of strange creatures: the orangutan, the armadillo, toucans and hornbills, as well as the improbable duck-billed platypus and echidna. Later the exotic, tropical dugong came into his purview. It was seldom that any weird or wonderful, strange or sensational creature that perished at the zoo, or in a private collection, escaped Owen's dissecting knife.

The striking, spectacular and odd of the invertebrate world also attracted him. In 1841 he marvelled at the intricate skeleton of a new sea sponge species that had been found in the Pacific Ocean. It resembled 'a delicate cornucopia', he wrote, composed of 'stiff, glistening, elastic threads, resembling the finest hairs of spun glass'. The skeleton is indeed made of glass-like silica, which supports the creature, *Euplectella aspergillum*, nicknamed 'Venus' flower basket'. The organism creates its lattice-like skeleton from materials extracted from seawater. Owen ended his description by saying, 'in the exquisite beauty and regularity of the texture of the walls of the cone, the species surpasses any of the allied productions that I have, as yet, seen, or found described.'[1]

From the small to the very large, gigantic extinct birds had held a fascination for Owen from early on in his career. While visiting the Netherlands in September 1838, he wrote to his wife, following a trip to a Dutch art gallery:

> What do you think I espied in a dark corner? Why, a DODO – a dodo in full plumage. Note that he (the artist or the dodo, whichever you please) lived between 1576 and 1639. He was contemporary with the man whom the Natural History credits as having brought the stuffed dodo from Mauritius.

Although he enjoyed looking at all the paintings in the gallery, mainly those by the Old Masters and those depicting religious subjects, Owen was first and foremost a comparative anatomist, and wrote of the dodo:

> The nostrils are very far forwards, as in the apteryx [kiwi], and the feet very similar in the relative position and size of the toes. I took a sketch; the head precisely resembles that of the Oxford specimen.[2]

Years later, in 1865, Owen was sent a parcel of bones 'found in a morass' by George Clark, a schoolmaster, and then forwarded by the Bishop of Mauritius. The bones proved to have been derived from several individuals, and some portions were missing. Nevertheless, he noted that the 'collection included most of the bones of the

Dodo, from copper plate in John Ray, ed., *The Ornithology of Francis Willughby* (1676).

skeleton and all those of importance for testing the hypotheses of the affinities and place in nature of this most strange and extinct bird'. The idea that the dodo of Mauritius and the rather similar solitaire from the nearby island of Rodrigues were related to doves and pigeons had been hypothesized in 1842 by the Danish naturalist Johannes Theodor Reinhardt (1816–1882), but the notion had initially been ridiculed, although it was later discovered to be well founded. Owen wrote to his sister that the dodo 'proves to be a great ground pigeon, grown too big to fly, and so let its wings go to waste'.[3] Owen developed his ideas more fully in a detailed memoir of the species in 1866:

> If the great Ground-dove of Mauritius gradually gained bulk in the long course of successive generations in that uninhabited thickly wooded island, and [was] exempt from attacks of any enemy, with food enough scattered over the ground, [and] ceased to exert the wing to raise the heavy trunk, then on Lamarck's principle, the disused members would atrophy, while the hind limbs, through increased exercise by habitual motion on land, with increasing weight to support, would hypertrophy.[4]

This passage not only shows an appreciation of the idea of adaptation to an environment and way of life but clearly also adopts an evolutionary approach: 'gradually . . . in the long course of successive generations . . .' clearly implies long-term change. Likewise, the suggestion that the wings could atrophy through disuse, and hind limbs 'through increased exercise . . . on land . . . would hypertrophy', implies a mechanism provided by 'the law of use and disuse'. Clearly, by this stage of his career, in this instance at least, Owen is something of an evolutionist, although he is careful to include himself in the Lamarckian camp, rather than among the Darwinists.

Around the time that one of his papers on the dodo was published, Owen wrote papers on several other strange and striking creatures: the aye-aye (an endemic nocturnal lemur from Madagascar), as well as another 'giant extinct bird' from Mauritius – the broad-billed parrot or raven parrot (*Psittacus mauritianus*, now referred to as *Lophopsittacus mauritianus*), which was a truly gigantic parrot that was up to 65 centimetres (25 ½ in.) in length, with a vast head, jaw and beak[5] – along with *Dinornis*, the enormous, flightless, extinct New Zealand moa.

The extinct Mauritius broad-billed parrot (*Lophopsittacus mauritianus*), described by Richard Owen in 1866, is seen on the left in this drawing by Thomas Herbert, 1634.

Owen had a reputation for being able to reconstruct the appearance of a long-extinct creature from a single bone or some other fossil fragment: this myth possibly overemphasized Owen's ability in this regard, but the story was not entirely without foundation. Owen's friend Cuvier had previously claimed to have this ability. Reconstructing an organism from tracks or footprints is perhaps analogous to doing so from a single bone, and Richard Owen suggested the name *Protichnites* for the fossil animal tracks sent to him from Canada. He correctly described them as being the oldest footprints found on land: they dated from the period that is now known as the Cambrian (a geological period that extended from about 540 to 485 million years ago). Owen applied his knowledge of anatomy and, after some hesitation, he suggested that they were made by 'articulates' (a group that included the arthropods, such as crabs and lobsters).[6] He suggested that there was some similarity to *Limulus*, the king crab. Over 150 years later, fossils of the creature that made the tracks were discovered, and he was seen to have been largely correct.

Sometime in the 1830s, a New Zealand trader by the name of John Harris acquired a fragment of bone of about 15 centimetres (6 in.) in length. In February 1837, it came into the hands of a retired naval surgeon, John Rule, who initially speculated that it might belong to a giant bird of prey. He carried the specimen with him to England, where it was offered for sale to the Hunterian Collection: the museum committee declined to buy it, and Owen himself could not afford the price suggested (10 guineas). Nevertheless, Owen retained custody of the bone, thereafter describing and drawing it. Gideon Mantell, the palaeontologist, later claimed that Owen had indicated that the specimen had been bought by the Hunterian Museum (and was thus the museum's property and within Owen's purview), whereas it had in fact been purchased by an individual. Mantell's rivalry with Owen was intense. He felt extremely strongly about Owen's deceit in this matter, as they had previously co-operated, and Mantell had given to Owen a box of bones from New Zealand, sent by his son, Walter.

In any event, in a publication in 1840, Owen claimed to have deduced the existence of a hitherto unknown giant, flightless bird in New Zealand from the evidence of this fragment of bone. His Zoological Society colleagues were initially sceptical, but Owen had realized that it could not have come from a flying species of bird; he risked his reputation by asserting 'that there has existed, if there does not now exist, in New Zealand, a Struthious bird nearly, if not quite, equal in size to the Ostrich'. (There are those who claim that Owen had heard about the folk traditions of the Maoris concerning a giant, flightless bird; thus the 'deduction' was not quite all that it seemed.)

Other moa bones were sent in due course from New Zealand by a missionary stationed there, William Williams. William John Broderip (1789–1859), a lawyer, naturalist and collector of curios, was present with Owen when one consignment was opened on 19 January 1843. Broderip wrote an account of the incident to Buckland in Oxford:

> I look upon it as the greatest zoological discovery of our time . . .
> We went over Owen's paper on the fragment of bone, the work of
> a man in the dark with the exception of the glimmering he could
> collect from that fragment. Every word comes true to the letter,
> and he had drawn the terminations of the imperfect bone on
> his copy of the plate, which might have been sketched from the
> perfect bone before us on the table.[7]

Broderip also detailed the experience in an article, which went on to be published anonymously in the popular *Penny Cyclopaedia* and, later, the rather more academically respectable *Quarterly Review*; it was from this that Owen's alleged ability to reconstruct an entire extinct creature from a single bone fragment was widely publicized.

In a series of papers published between 1844 and 1886, Owen wrote extensively on the moas. He coined the name *Dinornis*, derived from the Greek, meaning 'terrible bird'. He was correct, in that the largest moas were over 3 metres (10 ft) in height and probably, when alive, weighed up to 280 kilograms (617 lb); they

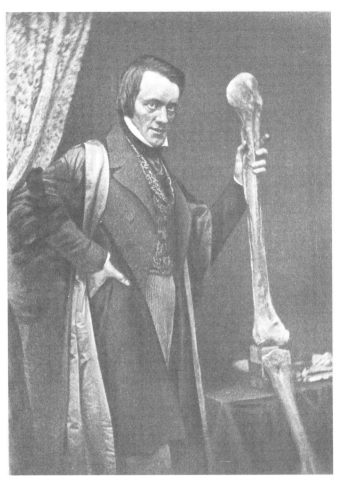

Richard Owen holding a moa femur and wearing the academic robes of the Hunterian Professor of the Royal College of Surgeons. Engraving based on a daguerreotype, 1846.

have claims to be the tallest bird that ever existed. They differ from other flightless birds in having no vestigial wings. At one time, more than thirty species were described, but the males and females were appreciably different in size, and some of the species described earlier as separate were probably the result of sexual dimorphism (differences between males and females). Today, nine species are recognized: *D. novaezealandae* from North Island and *D. robustus* from South Island, along with seven smaller species belonging to five genera. The group was rendered extinct through human hunting after the settlement of New Zealand by the Maoris in about 1300. Owen posed for a photograph that showed him in a full-length academic gown alongside an assembled moa skeleton.

Owen was evidently regarded, more or less throughout his life, as a legitimate target for the numerous inquirers as to the nature and habits of such fictional monsters as the cockatrice, the phoenix and the bunyip (this last monster being an imaginary creature that hailed from Australia, the skull of which turned out to be merely that of an embryonic sheep).[8]

In April 1855 a Turkish 'personage' called on Owen to ask him his opinion of the phoenix – a long-lived, immortal bird associated with classical mythology (although it has analogues in many cultures) that allegedly cyclically regenerates or is otherwise born again. A phoenix is said to obtain new life by arising from the ashes of its predecessor. Some legends say that it dies in a fiery burst of flames.

The 'personage', the servant of a Turkish Sultan, drew 'a most beautiful ladle, with a handle of carved coral and gold, jewelled' and a bowl made from a rose and cream horn-like material from inside his clothing, these being held to be carved from the beak of a phoenix. After some research in the museum, Richard Owen identified the head and beak of the bird that must have provided the material for the Sultan's ladle: the Asian helmeted hornbill (*Rhinoplax vigil*). Owen's visitor was greatly impressed. In passing, we may note that this species has a large red casque, or helmet, and a red throat, and sometimes flaps its wings in a kind of display. Its association with the legendary creature is thus perhaps understandable.[9]

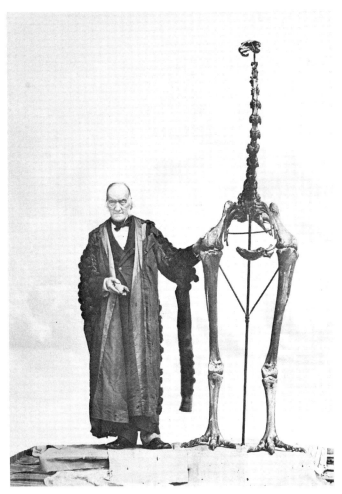

Richard Owen standing beside a complete moa (*Dinornis*) skeleton, *c.* 1877.

Asian helmeted hornbill (*Rhinoplax vigil*), late 19th century, engraving.

Another, more ancient bird, or bird-like creature, with which Richard Owen's name is often associated is *Archaeopteryx*. Sometimes referred to as the oldest bird – the name means 'ancient wing' – although older bird fossils have now been identified, and the creature is sometimes described as a bird-like dinosaur, it certainly has claims to be considered an intermediate creature between reptiles and true birds, having some of the characteristics of each of these groups. Its discovery a couple of years after the publication of Darwin's *On the Origin of Species* meant that it attracted enormous attention as a possible evolutionary missing link. The creature was first described from the fossil of a single feather, found in a limestone quarry near Solnhofen, in Bavaria, southern Germany, in 1861 (or possibly 1860). The name *Archaeopteryx lithographica* was given because of the specimen being found in a rock used for lithographic purposes. A more complete specimen was found near Langenaltheim (Middle Franconia). The specimen soon came into the possession of a local doctor, it is said, in payment for medical bills. Owen, who was always looking for spectacular and unique items to display in the museums for which he was responsible, decided that the British Museum must have it. (In addition, Owen was very competitive, especially when foreign interests were involved.) He sent one of his assistants, G. R. Waterhouse, to 'treaty for the collection of fossils, in which is the curious fossil with the alleged feathered vertebrate tail' in July 1862. Owen's wife, Caroline, wrote in her diary on 17 July 1862: 'The old German doctor is

The *Archaeopteryx* specimen unearthed in Germany and procured by Owen for the British Museum in London.

obstinate about his price, and Mr W has come away empty-handed. We ought not to lose the fossil.'[10]

They succeeded. Eventually £400 was paid for the strange fossil vertebrate, along with some two hundred other fossil specimens.[11] In 1863, a paper written by Owen appeared in *Transactions of the Royal Society,* in which he used the name *Archaeopteryx macrura*: he believed that it might not have been from the same species as the lone feather. However, Owen's specific choice of name does not find general acceptance today.

An attempt was made over a hundred years later by the distinguished Cambridge astronomer Sir Fred Hoyle (1915–2001), among others, to assert that the 'London specimen' was a forgery, masterminded by Owen. According to this interpretation, this deceit was perpetrated because Owen was strongly opposed to evolutionary ideas, and he thought that when the forgery was exposed, it would discredit the evolutionists. There is not the slightest evidence for this assertion: the London specimen and about a dozen other specimens have been intensively studied and are definitely genuine. The theory presupposes that Richard Owen was an anti-evolution creationist. This is an error: he was certainly of rather traditional Christian faith and, for much of the latter part of his career, he held an extreme personal dislike of Darwin and even more so of Darwin's friend, colleague and 'bulldog' Thomas Huxley. Certainly, there were times in his life when Owen adopted something of an evolutionary outlook, although it is true that in the early 1860s he had little time for the notion of natural selection as being the *mechanism* by which it came about.

Whatever Richard Owen's understanding of the evolutionary significance of *Archaeopteryx* in 1862, this was subordinate to his appreciation of its uniqueness and spectacular nature – and to its ability, when displayed in the British Museum, to 'attract the crowds' and bring prestige to the museum. This would, in turn, draw attention to him as the person responsible for securing this specimen for the museum, and, incidentally, for Britain. As early as 1842, while working on the Hunterian Collection, he had declaimed: 'Collections of natural objects, selected for their significance, rarity, or beauty have ever been regarded as the signs and ornaments of civilized nations; and . . . intellectual wealth.'[12] Acquiring the bizarre, unique 'feathered vertebrate', even at considerable (although perhaps not completely extravagant) cost, served the dual purposes of public education and boosting British prestige, as well as Owen's own self-gratification.

Other creatures that are often referenced by scientists discussing the evolution of the vertebrates include the lungfish, of which about six species now persist, although there are a larger number of fossil forms. The Queensland lungfish (*Neoceratodus forsteri*) is found only in Australia, although fossil records of this group date back about 380 million years, around the time when the higher vertebrates were beginning to evolve. Fossils of lungfish that were quite similar to this species have been uncovered in New South Wales, suggesting that the Queensland lungfish (or something like it) has existed in Australia for at least 100 million years. It could thus be described as a 'living fossil' and is one of the oldest living vertebrates, being the most primitive surviving member of the ancient air-breathing lungfish (Dipnoi) family. Moreover, lungfish have been found to be quite closely related to the tetrapods (amphibians, reptiles, mammals), since they breathe air and have a quite advanced skeletal structure.

Richard Owen described the African lungfish, suggesting the name *Lepidosiren annectens*: this fish is still referred to scientifically as *Protopterus annectens*.[13] In his detailed description of this creature (his specimen came from the River Gambia in West Africa) he remarked that the lungfish marked the 'nearest approach of the class of fishes to the . . . reptiles.' Once again, Owen showed considerable interest in organisms that were later found to be of importance in the development of evolutionary ideas.

Such activities – posing with the bones of giant birds, acquiring something unique from under the noses of the authorities of Britain's imperial rival, Germany, and writing about the weird, exotic and strange – did nothing to injure the high public profile that Richard Owen enjoyed for much of his career, which was enhanced by his careful cultivation of those with political influence.

From the 1830s onwards, Owen kept a scrapbook concerning giant creatures of a different character; because of his public reputation, he was often sent letters and other material concerning a range of strange creatures, including sea monsters. A notebook, now archived among the Owen papers held in the London Natural History Museum, bears the title: *Collection of Newspaper Cuttings Relating to the Alleged Appearance of the Sea-Serpent.*[14]

Stories of giant sea monsters or sea-serpents are as old as tales of the sea. They appear in legends around the world, from Norse mythology to classical writings from the Mediterranean basin. The first American sea-serpent was described close to Cape Ann, Massachusetts, in 1639, while 'a most dreadful monster' was seen off the coast of Greenland in 1734. Reports of giant marine creatures were not uncommon in the British press of the Victorian period. Typical of such reports was one from the crew of HMS *Daedalus*, under the command of Captain Peter M'Quhae. The men claimed to have seen a serpent-like creature pass close to their ship near the Cape of Good Hope, in the latter part of 1848. It was allegedly 9 to 12 metres in length (30–40 ft), with a mane like that of a horse

Artist's impression of the sea monster allegedly seen from HMS *Daedalus* in 1848, from *Illustrated London News*, 28 October 1848.

and a mouth full of 'jagged teeth'. On returning to Britain, Captain M'Quhae gave a detailed report to *The Times*, which was published on 9 October 1848. The *Illustrated London News* then provided an artist's impression. Owen replied in the 9 November 1849 edition of *The Times*, asserting that the creature had been misidentified. He later said that he thought the most likely explanation was a huge seal or sea lion, with a wake behind it, asserting the improbability or mistaken nature of earlier accounts. A common feature of 'all the stories and drawings of large sea serpents [was that] there was no undulation at all of the body, or else it is a vertical one, which is not characteristic of serpents.' He went on to say that no remains had ever been washed up on any coast; moreover,

> a serpent being an air-breathing animal, dives with an effort, and commonly floats when dead, and so would a sea-serpent, until decomposition or accident had opened the tough integument and let out the imprisoned gases . . . During life the exigencies of the respiration of the great sea-serpent would always compel him frequently to the surface; and, when dead and swollen, it would
> > Prone on the flood, extended long and large,
> > Lie floating many a rood.
> Such a spectacle, demonstrative of the species if it existed, has not hitherto met the gaze of any of the countless voyagers who have traversed the seas in so many directions.

Other reports of sea monsters trickled in. One came from the Duke of Northumberland: the drawing that was provided was identified by Owen as a ribbonfish (of the Trachipteridae family). Captain George Harrington, of the *Castilian*, reported a creature similar to the *Daedalus* monster off the island of St Helena in the South Atlantic in 1857. Yet another creature, described as being around 5 metres (16 ft) long, was washed up in Bermuda in 1860. This was later identified as an oarfish (Regalecidae), which is related to the ribbon fish.[15]

In 1877, no less a vessel than the Royal Yacht, HMS *Osborne*, was sailing off Sicily in the Mediterranean when there was yet another sighting; again reports were sent to Owen, but again he was dismissive, suggesting that the crew had probably seen some species of whale.

Prince Albert was drawn into the discussions at one stage. Owen had the honour of explaining his views to the Prince Consort when Albert attended one of Owen's lectures. The humorous magazine *Punch* published a parody:

> Who killed the sea-serpent?
> 'I,' said Professor Owen.

At one stage, Owen stated that there was more evidence for the existence of ghosts than of sea-serpents. He was always dismissive of such reports, including those by trustworthy observers, such as experienced naval officers, even when they appeared in statements or affidavits sworn before a magistrate or a similar person in authority. What Owen required was a physical specimen, such as a portion of skin or a vertebra. He argued that if sea-serpents existed, occasionally their carcasses would be cast ashore, and bones or even fossils would be found. Such an outlook coincided with his viewpoint that the only truly scientific approach was to insist upon a specimen; the legalistic approach, based on sworn statements and stamped reports, just would not be acceptable. Richard Owen was a museum-based naturalist for much of his career with the

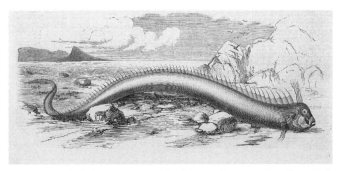

Oarfish that washed ashore on a Bermuda beach in 1860, from *Harper's Weekly*, 3 March 1860. The animal was 5 m (16 ft) long and was originally described as a sea-serpent.

Chang and Eng Bunker, the original 'Siamese twins', 1865.

Hunterian Collection, and later at the British Museum (Natural History). Museums, in his view, represented the most appropriate repositories of scientific knowledge. If an organism could not be dissected, preserved in spirit, catalogued, displayed, measured accurately and admired, it probably did not exist.

It would now be regarded as anything but politically correct, but Owen also, on occasion, expressed himself interested in oddities in the human form. His grandson remarked that 'he never let an opportunity pass of seeing with his own eyes any curious or abnormal development of the human frame.'[16] On one occasion, he asked to examine the bony, muscular fingers of the violinist and composer Heinrich Wilhelm Ernst (1812–1865).

In 1835 Richard Owen examined Chang and Eng (1811–1874), the original 'Siamese' conjoined twins, who were touring western Europe. They were joined at the base of the sternum, and Owen's examination was with a view to a possible severance. (He was then still involved in medical practice – he did not completely relinquish practising until early in 1837.) His opinion was that 'the operation would have been attended with imminent danger of peritonitis and death of probably both.' Unsurprisingly, 'the youths and their guardian objected' to separation.[17] It is almost certain that modern surgery techniques could have successfully separated them.

On 1 December 1864 Richard Owen was visited by 'General Tom Thumb', whose real name was Charles Sherwood Stratton (1838–1883) and his wife 'Mrs Thumb', Lavinia Warren Stratton (née Bump, 1842–1919); they were American dwarves who toured as circus performers, and who visited Queen Victoria and the Prince of Wales. A couple of years before, in August 1862, Owen went to see 'Joseph Brice, the French giant, now being exhibited in London'. He described Brice as 'quite a Goliath as he lay his full length, with his great hands spread out on a bed.' The idea that someone showing 'abnormal development' (he was around 2.3 metres (7 ft 6 in.) in height), unwell, in bed and apparently suffering from a cold, should be exhibited as a curiosity is quite abhorrent to modern tastes, but such 'entertainments' were regarded with slightly less revulsion in the Victorian era. Perhaps Owen, because of his professional and

General Tom Thumb (Charles Sherwood Stratton) and Mrs Thumb (aka Lavinia Warren Stratton, née Bump) as they appeared on the cover of *Harper's Weekly*, 21 February 1863, on the occasion of their wedding.

social standing, considered that his scientific approach placed him in a different situation from other visitors.

Richard Owen, through much of his professional life, was a controversialist. He appeared to positively relish rivalry and dispute – but he also liked to win, and enjoyed the discomfiture of a colleague with whom he disagreed. From his powerful stations within the College of Surgeons, the Zoological Society and St Bartholomew's Hospital, he was frequently in a position from whence he could dominate any opposition. He was a larger-than-life figure, to whom spectacular, exotic creatures and peculiar manifestations of the human form appealed.[18] It is the most spectacular monsters of all, the Mesozoic reptiles, and the controversies that they generated, to which we now turn.

4

Dr Owen, Dr Mantell
and the Dinosaurs

Perhaps the similarities that existed between Richard Owen and
Gideon Mantell were part of the reason for the rivalry that developed
between them. Although Mantell was the elder by fourteen years,
both started life relatively humbly, in provincial towns: Lewes in
Sussex, in the case of Mantell (born 3 February 1790). While Owen's
father was a merchant who had died when Richard was a small child,
Mantell's father was a shoemaker. Both men entered the medical
field through apprenticeship – Mantell was apprenticed to a local
apothecary-surgeon before completing his training, like Owen, in
London, qualifying at the Royal College of Surgeons in 1811. Both
moved from medicine and surgery to the field of natural history
(including geology), and both men became particularly interested
in fossils and the emerging science of palaeontology. Both were
exceptionally able and hard-working, Owen becoming a fellow of
the Royal Society at thirty, Mantell at 35, in 1825. Both were further
honoured by the Royal Society later in life. Perhaps because of their
relatively humble backgrounds, both also had a propensity to seek
out the influential, the powerful and the aristocratic: one biographer
referred to Mantell as 'a social climber, parvenu and sycophant'.
Mantell, at one point, described Owen as 'overpaid, overpraised and
with a jealous monopolising spirit'.[1] Both were excellent lecturers,
advancing their careers by giving popular lectures to the general
public. In addition, both were interested in fossil reptiles, which have
always been and still are creatures that capture the imagination.

Gideon Mantell had wandered around the quarries and
coastal cliffs of Sussex since his teenage years and had amassed an

impressive collection of fossils – ammonites, echinoids (sea urchins) and fish. By the 1820s, he was discovering much larger fossils – those of vertebrates. In 1822 Mantell (or perhaps his wife, Mary Ann, née Woodhouse, whom he had married in 1816) found a series of larger teeth that he identified as those of reptiles: initially, scientific opinion differed as to both their age and nature: some suggested that they were, in fact, from fish or mammals. After some discussion and the circulation of some of the specimens to other scientists, it was agreed that they were those of a large herbivorous reptile; in 1825 Mantell published a paper in *Philosophical Transactions*, the prestigious journal of the Royal Society, entitled 'Notice on the Iguanodon, a Newly Discovered Fossil Reptile, from the Sandstone of Tilgate, in Sussex'. Further collections of fossil reptiles in the South of England, and their comparison with those from elsewhere, resulted in his penning an essay, 'The Geological Age of Reptiles'; this was semi-popular in tone, and initially appeared in the *Sussex Advertiser*. It was reprinted in the *Edinburgh New Philosophical Journal* and thereby came to the notice of a wider group of scientists.[2] The first paragraph is worth reproducing, substantially:

Among the numerous interesting facts which the researches of modern geologists have brought to light, there is none more extraordinary and imposing than the discovery that there was a period when *the earth was peopled by oviparous quadrupeds of an almost appalling magnitude*, and that reptiles were *Lords of Creation*, before the existence of the human race! These creatures of the ancient world, many of which [were of] extraordinary size and form . . . existed in immense numbers. Their remains occur in strata far more ancient than those which contain the reliquiae of viviparous animals [mammals] and are found in marine as well as in fresh water deposits. Some of them, from their organization, have evidently been fitted to live in the sea only, while others were terrestrial, and many were inhabitants of lakes and rivers. The animal and vegetable remains with which the fossil bones are associated belong to a very different order of things from that in which the modern oviparous quadrupeds

S. Stepney, after J. J. Masquerier, *Gideon Mantell*, 1837, engraving.

are placed; and we are compelled to conclude that the condition of the earth, at the period it was peopled by reptiles, must have been very different from its present state.

The article described the 'enormous herbivorous reptiles', that is, the *Iguanodon* and the *Plesiosaurus*, as well as pterodactyls and the *Megalosaurus*, in relation to the geological strata in which they were to be found and their probable habitat.

Mantell ended the essay as follows: 'With the chalk, the "age of reptiles" may be said to terminate . . . the crocodiles, turtles &c

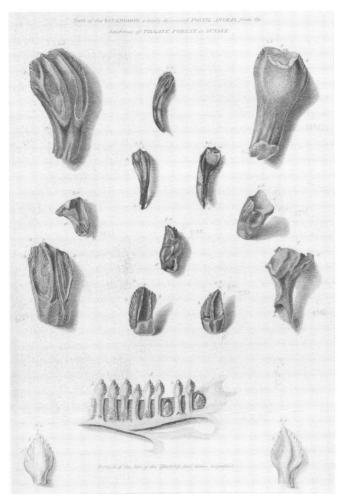

The teeth of *Iguanodon*, from Gideon Mantell, 'Notice on the Iguanodon, a newly discovered fossil reptile, from the sandstone of Tilgate Forest, in Sussex', *Philosophical Transactions of the Royal Society of London*, cxv (1825).

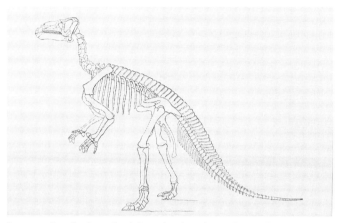

Reconstruction of an *Iguanodon* skeleton, found in Belgium, showing the probable bipedal posture, from Othniel Charles Marsh, *The Dinosaurs of North America* (1896).

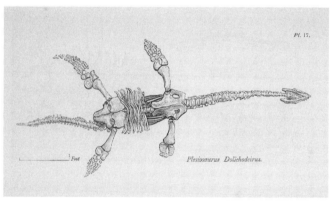

Reconstruction of a plesiosaur (fossil marine reptile), from William Buckland, *Geology and Mineralogy Considered with Reference to Natural Theology* (1836).

alone survived, a new order of things commenced, and in the tertiary formations which succeeded, we perceive an approach to the modern conditions of the earth.' Although the notion of a period in which reptiles were important had been hinted at by the French comparative anatomist and palaeontologist Cuvier, it was

Gideon Mantell who placed the idea of the 'Age of Reptiles' into the popular imagination. Moreover, in indicating the nature of the other life forms with which the Mesozoic reptiles were associated, and the conditions under which they lived, he could be said to have pioneered palaeoecology. Mantell followed up this article with a two-volume work, *The Wonders of Geology*, in 1838; this was a remarkably detailed summary, based on a series of lectures delivered in Brighton, in which other fossil reptiles were identified and described.[3]

However, the unfortunate Mantell had not reckoned with the abilities and somewhat oblique character of Richard Owen. Although Owen had written several papers on palaeontology before, he only settled into his work on fossils in about 1838. In that year he wrote a short paper on an *Ichthyosaurus* (a fish-like marine reptile), and 'A description of a specimen of the *Plesiosaurus macrocephalus* in the collection of Viscount Cole' was published. Owen could seldom resist the possibility of associating with the aristocracy. However, the person who actually found the specimen, Mary Anning, a self-educated woman and a renowned fossil hunter, was not mentioned (this was far from atypical at the time). During 1839, Owen, Buckland and William Conybeare (1787–1857, later dean of Llandaff) visited Lyme Regis in Dorset – from whence many early reptile fossils had come – as a group, so that Anning could lead them on a fossil-collecting expedition. Gideon Mantell had also worked with her.

Richard Owen was well positioned to develop his research, due to his connections with the Royal Society and the British Association for the Advancement of Science: he obtained funding support from the latter (1838–46) for his extensive work on British fossil reptiles (all this was happening while the sorting, classification and writing-up of the Hunterian Collection continued, not to mention the cascade of other comparative anatomy papers that fell from Owen's pen). This research involved perusing the writings of Conybeare and his friend and mentor Buckland (the Canon of Christ Church, Oxford), as well as Gideon Mantell; he also inspected materials from various museums around Britain (and on the continent). The first of a two-volume set of reports appeared in 1839 and the second in 1841 – both published by the British Association for the Advancement of Science. Both volumes are full of detail and contain descriptions of many new species: the first contains descriptions of sixteen plesiosaur species and ten ichthyosaurs. The second report is perhaps more important; as well as accounts of crocodiles, turtles and lizards, it contains descriptions of two genera that had been described by Mantell (*Iguanodon* and *Hylaeosaurus*) and one described by Buckland (*Megalosaurus*), grouping them all in a new order and coining the term *dinosaur*, or 'terrible lizard'.

It has been argued that this flurry of activity had the effect of deflecting attention from Mantell's work, for example, Mantell's account of the *Iguanodon*, with its spectacular illustrations, in his *Wonders of Geology.* Indeed, Owen effectively plagiarized some of Mantell's writings, claiming credit for work that was not his own, as well as, perhaps deliberately, misquoting him.

Gideon Mantell replied almost immediately to Owen's report in a very deferential, almost obsequious, letter to the *Literary Gazette*, drawing attention to what he saw as Owen's unfairness:

> But while expressing my admiration of the report, I beg permission to comment on a few statements which are not quite correct, and which from my personal knowledge of the liberal and honourable conduct of the highly gifted author towards his predecessors in the field of research, in which he has acquired such deserved reputation, I am persuaded from inadvertence or misapprehension.[4]

Mantell then listed several instances wherein Owen appeared to have ignored or misquoted his work on *Iguanodon*, *Hylaeosaurus* and fossil turtles. Mantell ended the letter by referring to Owen as

> the illustrious palaeontologist whose courtesy and liberality I have so often experienced, and who has noted my humble labours in terms sufficiently flattering to satisfy one far more solicitous of honourable mention than

Sir, you obedient servant
Gideon Algernon Mantell.

The obsequiousness did not placate Owen, who continued his persecution of Mantell until the latter's death, and indeed after.

Mantell, meanwhile, had fallen on hard times: in 1833 he had removed to Brighton, perhaps to be closer to the 'social scene', and his medical practice suffered. He was forced to sell his fossil collection in 1838 – it was bought for £4,000 by the British Museum, and thus became available to Owen. A further move to Clapham in south London followed, and he attempted to re-establish his medical practice. Despite his trials, Mantell continued his palaeontological research and clearly continued to be upset by his treatment at the hands of Owen.

To be fair, Mantell was probably not the easiest person with whom to get along. He had filled the elegant drawing room (and, apparently, every other room) of his substantial residence in Lewes with bones and fossils, to the annoyance of his long-suffering wife. Mantell also seems to have made a number of poor business decisions. His wife Mary left him in 1839, and in the same year, his son emigrated to New Zealand, from whence, incidentally, he sent numerous fossil specimens, including those of the moa. His daughter Hannah died a year later.

Misfortune continued to befall Mantell. In 1841 he suffered a severe carriage accident on Clapham Common. He seems to have fallen from his seat and became entangled in the horse's reins, and then to have been dragged along the ground, after which his spine was damaged. He moved house once again in 1844, this time to Pimlico, where, racked by constant pain, he began to take opium. His personal diary (published in 1940) showed an intensifying dislike of Owen; one entry reads: 'It is deeply to be deplored that this eminent and gifted man can never act with candour and liberality.'

Possibly deliberately, on 10 November 1852 Gideon Mantell overdosed and lapsed into a coma, dying a few hours later. A post-mortem examination revealed that he suffered from scoliosis, or deformation of the spine. As a final insult, Owen somehow got hold of Mantell's spine; he had it preserved in spirit and displayed at the College of Surgeons.

But Owen was still not satisfied. Three days after Mantell's death, Owen published an obituary in the *Literary Gazette*. When listing Mantell's achievements and publications – from which any reference to 'The Age of Reptiles' was omitted – Owen damned Mantell with faint praise:

> Dr Mantell . . . was a most attractive lecturer, filling the listening ears of his audience with seductive imagery, and leaving them in amazement with his exhaustless catalogue of wonders. This, indeed, was his failing in a philosophic point of view. He yielded with reluctance to the revelation of a truth when it dispossessed him of a pretty illustration . . . To touch lightly on other weaknesses of this enthusiastic diffuser of geological knowledge, too prominent and too generally understood to be passed over by the impartial biographer, we must notice the intrinsic want of exact scientific, especially anatomical knowledge, which compelled him to have recourse to those possessing it.[5]

The president of the Geological Society wrote that the obituary 'bespeaks of the lamentable coldness of heart'.

Owen's reputation, however, went from strength to strength on the basis of the *Reports* (described as a tour de force) and a steady trickle of descriptions of other fossil reptiles followed.

In the same year that the unfortunate Mantell perished, the Crystal Palace, which was built for the Great Exhibition of 1851, was moved from Hyde Park to a permanent site in Sydenham. It was suggested by Prince Albert that models of some of the ancient reptiles should decorate the grounds. Somewhat fanciful, life-sized representations were sculpted by a Mr Benjamin Waterhouse Hawkins: these huge sculptures overemphasized the real dinosaurs' size and ferociousness. One comment was that 'the animals like the geologists seem to have been engaged in combat.' Inside the hollow sculpture of the *Iguanodon*, on New Year's Eve, 1853, a group of 22 distinguished persons – the sculptor and a number of

View of the gardens at the Crystal Palace, with five large models of dinosaurs in the foreground, print by George Baxter, 1854.

men of science – gathered for a formal dinner. Professor Owen, unsurprisingly, was at the head of the table. An illustration of the event appeared in the *Illustrated London News*; Owen seldom missed an opportunity for publicity. However, although Mantell had shown that the *Iguanodon*, along with certain other dinosaurs, were bipedal, Owen's instructions to the sculptor resulted in the creature at Crystal Palace being massively oversized and quadripedal.

By 'inventing' the dinosaurs, or at least distinguishing them as a biological group with their own easily remembered name and their own identity, publicizing their existence to the scientific community with his *Report of British Fossil Reptiles* – and more generally, by the New Year's Eve dinner in 1853 (which was widely covered by the press) – Owen appropriated the spectacular creatures as his own creation. It would be his name that was remembered, rather than the pioneering work in the quarries of the South Downs conducted by Mantell. In 1878, the excavation of skeletons in good condition on the continent showed that the

Dinner presided over by Richard Owen, for a group of eminent men of science inside the model of the *Iguanodon*, New Year's Eve, 1853. Wines were served aplenty, and the dinner became quite 'boisterous' as the evening wore on. The above is how the event was recorded in the *Illustrated London News*, 7 January 1854.

Iguanodon was generally bipedal, along with other early dinosaurs. Mantell had been correct, but on this point, Owen was silent. He was a man who seldom acknowledged his errors or retracted anything that he had written.

5

Darwin and Owen

When Darwin returned to England from his voyages aboard HMS *Beagle*, Owen was already well established in his scientific career and had been awarded a Fellowship of the Royal Society two years previously, in 1834. The two men were naturally drawn to each other – perhaps owing to their similarities in background. They met, possibly only for the second time, for a tea party at the home of the geologist Charles Lyell and his wife, a matter of days after Darwin arrived in London on his return from the *Beagle* voyage, on 29 October 1836. They met regularly and often corresponded. Darwin attended lectures that were given by Owen, and they co-operated quite extensively on the description of some of the specimens garnered on the *Beagle* voyage; Owen was responsible for volume I of *The Zoology of the Voyage of HMS Beagle: Fossil Mammalia* (1838). Both men retained an interest in South American fossil mammals (some of which were classified as 'monsters') throughout much of their careers and, for a while, corresponded with one another on the subject when new information or novel specimens appeared. It has even been suggested that there was a certain symbiosis between Darwin, the field naturalist, and Owen, the museum and laboratory man, and also that there were certain sections of the *Origin* that might, just possibly, have been written with critique from Owen in mind.[1]

The co-operation between Darwin and Owen over the mammal fossils collected on the voyage of the *Beagle* ushered in a period in which Owen developed a strong interest in South American fossils: he published papers on a giant armadillo (*Glyptodon*) in 1839, and on *Mylodon*, an extinct gigantic sloth, in 1842.

A number of letters between the two men on various natural history subjects exist from this period (the late 1830s and early 1840s). For example, Owen dissected a bird specimen of a species that Darwin suspected might be nocturnal in its feeding; he asked Owen to determine whether it might, possibly, have a very sensitive sense of touch. When Darwin sent him a copy of his published *Journal* (the book now known as *The Voyage of the 'Beagle'*), Owen's reply was particularly effusive and light-hearted, being written hurriedly late in the evening:

> College of Surgeons
> June 11th, 1839
>
> Dear Darwin,
> I have read far enough into your Journal to feel that I have to thank you for the most delightful book in my collection. It is as full of good original wholesome food as an egg & if what I have enjoyed has not been duly digested it is because it has been too hastily devoured. I leave it reluctantly – tired eyes compelling at night, and greet it as a new luxury at the breakfast table.
> Ever your faithful & obliged, Richd. Owen.[2]

Mrs Owen's diary confirms that, for example, in the latter part of 1841, the Darwins and the Owens saw quite a lot of each other:[3]

> October 31. – Mr Darwin here to breakfast.
> November 10. – With R[ichard] to Gower St to see Mr and Mrs Darwin. Mr D had his arm in a sling.
> 15th. After dinner this evening, Mrs Darwin, Mr Gould and his brother came here for some music.[4]

Meanwhile, one of Darwin's associates had warned him about Owen, telling him that someday he would see the man's true nature.

After he had moved to Downe in Kent, in September 1842, Darwin wrote in the friendliest terms to Owen, inviting him to come with his wife and child (William) for a weekend of 'rest & air in the country'. The two families regularly sent Christmas greetings

Charles Darwin, *c*. 1855, while relations with Richard Owen were still cordial.

to each other. It is clear that Charles Darwin had the very greatest respect for Owen; the affection seems to have been mutual and continued for some years – they 'took tea' with each other from time to time.

An indication of the mutual respect in which they held each other is to be found in a note that Darwin wrote to his wife on 5 July 1844. He had just completed his essay in which he set out the bare bones of his 'species theory' and was concerned that if he were to die suddenly, the ideas it contained would be lost. In the letter, he asked his wife, in that eventuality, to allocate £400 to publishing the work, naming several scientists who might undertake the task of editing it. He wrote: 'Professor Owen would be very good; but I presume he would not undertake such a work.' Interestingly, the sentence was deleted at a later date.[5]

Owen strongly approved of Darwin's publication *Coral Reefs* (1842), and later wrote favourably of the work in *A Manual of Scientific Enquiry*, a book for travellers and voyagers. Darwin replied, in a letter that was apparently written in April 1848 (Darwin had probably seen Owen's remarks at the proof stage), saying how pleased he was to have Owen's approval.

Darwin published his monumental works on barnacles (Cirripedia) between 1851 and 1854, having corresponded with Owen about certain aspects of some of the specimens on which it was based.[6] Owen wrote a very appreciative letter on 17 July 1854, to which Darwin replied stating how gratified he was to receive it. Good relations continued; in a letter written in December 1854, Owen commented: 'I met with a very interesting party a few days ago at breakfast at Sir Robert Inglis's – the new President of the Royal Society, Lord Wrottesley, Sir J Herschel, Mr Robert Brown, Captain FitzRoy, Mr Charles Darwin (who went round the world with Captain F), Dean Morier.'[7] Meeting for breakfast seems to have been fashionable in scientific circles at the time.

At the opening of the Crystal Palace, after it had been moved from central London to Sydenham in 1854, on 20 April 1855, the Owens met 'Mr and Mrs Charles Darwin' there, when 'we walked about a bit with them'.

However, this bonhomie did not last. Following Darwin's receipt of a letter containing Wallace's draft of his ideas on evolution through natural selection, Darwin's friends and colleagues – Charles Lyell, a geologist, and Joseph Hooker, a botanist – arranged for short summaries of the evolutionary ideas of both Charles Darwin and Alfred Russel Wallace to be presented to a meeting of the Linnean Society of London in the summer of 1858; these were subsequently published together in the *Journal* of the Society. Owen referred,

Charles Lyell, geologist and friend of Charles Darwin, c. 1843–7.

quite positively, to this publication in his presidential address to the British Association for the Advancement of Science in that same year.

On the Origin of Species was published in November 1859, and Darwin had a presentation copy sent to Owen with a very friendly letter, albeit one acknowledging that there would be much in the book with which Owen would not agree. Owen acknowledged receipt at once, thanking Darwin for his 'kind recollection', and complimenting him on its publication. The letter concluded: 'For the application of your rare gifts to the solution of this supreme question, I shall ever feel my very great indebtedness.'

Darwin appears to have met Owen in London in early December 1859. However, the meeting seems to have been slightly strained. In an account of the meeting in a letter to Charles Lyell, Darwin described Owen as behaving 'with a degree of arrogance I never

Joseph Dalton Hooker, director of Kew Gardens, Charles Darwin's friend and opponent of Richard Owen, *c.* 1855.

saw approached' and being 'bitter and sneering against me'. Nevertheless, Darwin and Owen exchanged several reasonably good-natured letters over the next few days.

Not altogether unsurprisingly, Owen's letter upon his receipt of *On the Origin*, and some of his subsequent correspondence, seem to have lulled Darwin into a false sense of security.

ON

THE ORIGIN OF SPECIES

BY MEANS OF NATURAL SELECTION,

OR THE

PRESERVATION OF FAVOURED RACES IN THE STRUGGLE
FOR LIFE.

By CHARLES DARWIN, M.A.,

FELLOW OF THE ROYAL, GEOLOGICAL, LINNÆAN, ETC., SOCIETIES;
AUTHOR OF 'JOURNAL OF RESEARCHES DURING H. M. S. BEAGLE'S VOYAGE
ROUND THE WORLD.'

LONDON:

JOHN MURRAY, ALBEMARLE STREET.

1859.

Title page of Charles Darwin, *On the Origin of Species* (1859).

However, at this point, things changed. Owen reviewed *On the Origin* anonymously in the prestigious *Edinburgh Review* in 1860.[8] The review is a blend of damning with faint praise, sarcasm, the use of 'weasel words' and personal invective. It was clear at once who was the author: among other evidence was the fact that the review favourably mentioned three of Owen's own books.

Early in the review, a touch of jealousy emerges when the author cynically refers to 'Mr Darwin': 'Of independent means, he has full command of his time for the prosecution of original research.' He continues: 'Our younger naturalists have been seduced into acceptance of Mr Darwin's views.' Conversely, the views of 'Professor' Owen are quoted favourably. Is there not an element of self-aggrandizement here? The author speaks of *Professor* Owen, but of *Mr* Darwin. The review is many pages in length; many of the sentences are extremely long and, in places, convoluted, but the aim is clear – to ridicule and denigrate the views of Darwin, Wallace and their disciples, such as Thomas Huxley.

In the opening pages of *On the Origin*, Darwin described how he had been 'struck with certain facts in the distribution of the inhabitants of South America' while on the *Beagle* voyage, 'and in the geological relations of the present and past inhabitants of the continent'. He continues: 'These facts seemed to me to throw some light on the origin of species – that mystery of mysteries.'

Darwin was clearly referring to the similarities between the fossils of the continent and certain modern animals. However, Owen initially pretends not to understand: 'What is there, we asked ourselves, as we closed the volume to ponder on this paragraph – what can there be in the inhabitants of South America . . . to have suggested to any mind that man might be a transmuted ape or to throw any light on the origin of the human or any other species?' He also states: 'The scientific world has looked forward with great interest to the facts which Mr Darwin might *deem* adequate to the support of his theory on the supreme question of biology' (emphasis added).

Owen goes on, almost sneeringly, to state that the reader must assume that it must be Darwin's

superior grasp of mind, strength of intellect, clearness and
precision of thought and expression which raise one man so
far above his contemporaries as to enable him to discern in
the common stock of facts, of coincidences, correlations and
analogies in Natural History deeper and truer conclusions than
his fellow-labourers have been able to reach.

Later, he comments: 'Prosaic minds are apt to bore one by asking
for our proofs,' although *On the Origin* is crammed with examples
providing evidence for the theory of evolution through natural
selection. He goes on: 'Mr Darwin rarely refers to the writings of his
predecessors,' which was of course absolute nonsense.

After noting the reticence of Cuvier to discuss certain aspects of
the inheritance of characteristics, he continues: 'But the barrier at
which Cuvier hesitated, Mr Darwin rushes through.'

Thomas Huxley, who later became known as 'Darwin's Bulldog'
for his dogged defence of Charles Darwin's ideas, gave a lecture
stoutly defending *On the Origin* at the Royal Institution in February
1860 (five years earlier, in the same place, he had given a lecture that
was very sceptical regarding transmutation).

Owen included this gem in his *On the Origin* review:

But when the members of the Royal Institution of Great Britain
are taught by their evening lecturer that such a limited or
inadequate view and treatment of the great problem exemplifies
that application of science to which England owes its greatness,
we take leave to remind the managers that it more truly parallels
the abuse of science to which a neighbouring nation, some
seventy years since, owed its temporary degradation. By their
fruits may promoters of true and false philosophy be known.
We gazed with amazement at the audacity of the dispenser of
the hour's intellectual amusement, who, availing himself of the
technical ignorance of the majority of the auditors, sought to
blind them as to the frail foundations of 'natural selection'.

According to Owen, Huxley's giving a public lecture on the doctrine of evolution through natural selection was apparently 'an abuse of science', an evil that was comparable with the 'degradation' associated with the French Revolution. (Interestingly, relations between Owen and Huxley had previously been almost as congenial as those between Owen and Darwin. In 1851, Owen had written a letter of support for Huxley's unsuccessful application for the position of professor of natural history at the University of Toronto.)

Owen's review of *On the Origin*, which was many thousands of words in length, must be one of the longest and most vicious reviews printed in any respectable journal in the nineteenth century. Its publication affected Darwin deeply. In a letter to his old friend and teacher John Henslow on 8 May 1860, he wrote: 'he is mad with envy because my book has been talked about: what a strange man to be envious of a naturalist like myself, immeasurably his inferior!'[9]

However, a few weeks later, another anonymous review appeared, this time in the *Quarterly Review*, and was equally critical. Again, it eventually became clear who had written it: the author was Samuel Wilberforce, the Bishop of Oxford, who had apparently been assisted by Owen. Bishop Wilberforce was the same individual who engaged in the famous debate with Thomas Huxley over Darwin's ideas at the British Association for the Advancement of Science in Oxford, in late June 1860, with, according to Joseph Hooker, 'inimitable spirit, ugliness & emptiness & unfairness'. Hooker continued, in his letter of 2 July 1860: 'I saw he was coached up by Owen.'[10]

Darwin assumed that Owen was opposed to the idea of transmutation in itself, but the issue was almost certainly more complicated than that. In Chapter Nine of *On the Origin*, titled 'The Imperfection of the Geological Record', Darwin notes the extreme rarity of 'numerous transitional links between the many species that now exist or have existed', admitting that this is an objection 'of the gravest nature'. He continues: 'We see this in the plainest manner by the fact that all the most eminent palaeontologists, namely, Cuvier, Owen, Agassiz, Barrande, Falconer, E. Forbes &c . . . have unanimously, often vehemently, maintained the immutability of species.'

It is worth making the point here that transmutationist ideas were already very much in circulation: Charles Darwin's grandfather, Erasmus, the Frenchman Lamarck, Robert Chambers, who anonymously authored the book *Vestiges of the Natural History of Creation* (1844), and Darwin's own mentor in Edinburgh, Robert Edmond Grant, had all voiced evolutionary thoughts in print. Although much of Owen's antagonism was due to jealousy – Owen could see that he was no longer king of the English scientific castle – he opined that Darwin had misrepresented his views. Owen seemed to be saying that he was not the strict creationist that Darwin (and others) had claimed him to be. It is true that Owen had expressed views that were vaguely transmutationist, although they were very vague, especially in the 1850s.

After the pre-Christmas 1859 confrontation and Owen's dastardly 'anonymous' review, there was no possibility of reconciliation between the former friends. Many subsequent letters written by Darwin illustrate his antipathy: in a missive to Hooker on 25 January 1862, he declaims 'I am ashamed how demoniacal my feelings are towards Owen.' Hooker replied, a few days later: 'My only care is to avoid Owen – I can see now that he hates me with an intense hate.'

Owen prophesied that *On the Origin* would be forgotten in ten years.[11] He was, of course, wrong, but the antipathy between Sir Richard Owen and Darwin, his 'bulldog' Huxley and their associates, such as Joseph Hooker, was lifelong.

The ill-feeling between Owen and Huxley was particularly vicious – carried on in public, in lecture-halls and in the pages of journals, such as the *Natural History Review* and the *Athenaeum*. Owen had argued against the origin of humans from an ape-like ancestor, claiming that the gorilla's brain differed from the human brain in not having a structure known as a hippocampus minor. Humans, therefore, were anatomically quite distinct from the apes and should in no sense be classified with them. In this argument, Owen was found to be in error. The Darwinians, led by Huxley, gloated.

Sometimes, early in his career, Darwin used to defend Owen to his friends, some of whom had a very poor opinion of him. Looking back from late in life, Darwin recalled that Hugh Falconer had said: 'You will find him out one day,' and so it proved.[12] In 1860 Darwin noted in a letter to Falconer following the Oxford debate: 'I do heartily enjoy Owen having a good setting down – his arrogance and malignity are too bad.'[13]

In 1871 Owen was involved in a plan to end funding for the herbarium at Kew, which was supervised by Darwin's friend Joseph Hooker, and to have it brought under the control of the British Museum, where Owen was by then in charge of the natural history collections. Darwin wrote: 'I used to be ashamed of hating him so much, but now I will carefully cherish my hatred and contempt to the last days of my life.'[14]

The antagonism of Huxley towards Owen was possibly even greater than that between Darwin and Owen, or between Owen and Hooker. They shared the aim of the establishment of science as a profession and the importance of their own positions within it, so perhaps the rivalry was not altogether surprising. Huxley sought with 'evangelical fervour to establish a scientific status for natural history, to rid the discipline of women, amateurs, and parsons, and to place a secular science at the centre of cultural life in Victorian England'.[15]

Was the enmity between Darwin and Owen partly a matter of class, or, at least, of the perception of class? Owen was certainly not working-class, but he had rather different formative years from those of Darwin: he was apprenticed to a series of apothecary-surgeons in northern England, in comparison to the Cambridge background of Charles Darwin (both had spent some time at Edinburgh Medical School, but Owen's time there was only for a few months). Darwin's close friend and confidant Joseph Dalton Hooker was not Oxbridge-educated (as many of the Darwin party were, although not Wallace or Huxley) but he had been to Glasgow University, and he married (first) Frances Harriet Henslow (1825–1874), daughter of Darwin's friend and mentor, the Reverend John Stevens Henslow, professor of botany at Cambridge. On her death,

Richard Owen, *c*. 1855. He enjoyed lecturing in and being photographed in full
academic dress.

he married Lady Hyacinth Jardine (1842–1921), daughter of William
Samuel Symonds (like Darwin, of Christ's College, Cambridge) and
the widow of Sir William Jardine (7th Baronet of Applegarth,
1800–1874).

This might explain why Owen particularly esteemed the
Oxbridge contacts that he did have. Canon William Buckland
of Christ Church, Oxford, for one – geologist, theologian and

palaeontologist – was something of a mentor.[16] Owen may have had an affinity with him, not only because they shared an interest in fossil reptiles but because both were larger-than-life figures, outgoing in the promotion of their views and somewhat histrionic, almost flamboyant, in the lecture-hall. Buckland, like Richard Owen, did not get on well with Darwin, who described him as 'a vulgar and almost coarse man' and one driven 'more by a craving for notoriety, which sometimes made him behave like a buffoon, than by a love of science.'[17]

6

Huxley, the Hippocampus
and Histrionics

The tale of the development of evolutionary ideas is littered
with instances of coincidence, serendipity and contrast. Darwin
entrusted his fossil vertebrate specimens, gathered on the voyage
of HMS *Beagle*, to Richard Owen, on his return from his five years
a-voyaging; much later they came to detest one another. Early in
the career of Thomas Henry Huxley (1825–1895), Owen wrote a
testimonial in support; later there was a vicious and venomous
rivalry, amounting almost to hatred, between them. However, when
Owen's grandson – also named Richard – came to write a biography
of his grandfather, very soon after Sir Richard's death in 1894, he
called upon Thomas Huxley to assess Owen's position in science
in an Appendix.[1] The acknowledgement is worth quoting here: 'I
gladly take this opportunity of expressing my sincere gratitude to
the Right Hon. T. H. Huxley for the kind and generous contribution
he has made to the book, showing Professor Owen's position
in the history of anatomical science.'[2] The Appendix is far from
uncritical, but the fact that it exists at all suggests that some sort of
reconciliation must have occurred between the family and Huxley,
the staunchest critic of Owen's ideas.

There were similarities between Huxley and Owen, although
Huxley was twenty years younger. They both came from relatively
modest backgrounds – Huxley left school at twelve, after only a
couple of years of schooling. Both had entered the scientific field
after obtaining medical qualifications, both were exceptionally
hard-working and brilliant, specializing in comparative anatomy,
and both sought to promote the idea of the professional scientist

Thomas Henry Huxley with sketch of a gorilla skull, *c.* 1861.

– perhaps Huxley did this with greater vigour than Owen, who had his network of friends among the aristocracy, some of whom were keen amateur naturalists.

Huxley, to repay some of the debts that he had accumulated as a student, took the position of assistant surgeon on board HMS *Rattlesnake*, on her exploration voyage to Australia and New Guinea. In 1851, shortly after his return to London, Huxley wrote to an Australian naturalist colleague: 'It is astonishing [with] what an intense feeling of hatred Owen is regarded by the majority of his contemporaries, with Mantell as an arch-hater. The truth is he is superior to most, and does not conceal that he knows it, and it must be confessed that he does some very ill-natured tricks now and then.'[3]

Although there had clearly been skirmishes before, a significant deepening of the antagonism between Owen and Huxley was begun at the Oxford meeting of the British Association for the Advancement of Science in the autumn of 1860. Richard Owen was not present at the 'Great Debate' between Bishop Samuel Wilberforce and Thomas Huxley, although he *was* present at the annual meeting of the British Association for the Advancement of Science. It is likely that Owen coached Wilberforce before the debate; perhaps he deliberately avoided what he knew was likely to become a confrontation. He was, however, present at the presentation of a paper given in the Botany Section on the sexuality of plants. In this, the Oxford professor of botany, Charles Daubeny, was somewhat sympathetic to Darwin's ideas but was not unreservedly so. A vigorous discussion took place after the presentation. Owen claimed 'that the brain of a gorilla presented more differences as compared to that of a man, than it did when compared with the very lowest and most problematical of the Quadrumana [a former term for the division of mammals that includes the monkeys, apes and lemurs]'. In particular, he claimed that the human brain possessed a hippocampus (a small but complex brain structure embedded deep into the temporal lobe that has a major role in learning and memory), whereas other monkeys and apes did not. Huxley immediately contradicted this assertion, backing up his views in print the following year. In a piece entitled 'On the Zoological Relations between Man and the Lower Animals' in the *Natural History Review*, Huxley tried to demonstrate that the brain of the gorilla is more similar to that of the human than it is to other Quadrumana (higher primates).

The argument went on in the periodicals, claim against counterclaim, concerning minute details of the brain structure in the brains of humans and other primates. In a lecture to the Royal Institution, entitled 'The Gorilla and the Negro', Owen again emphasized the marked differences between the gorilla brain and that of the human, going into considerable technical detail. The lecture was reported in the *Athenaeum*, but in a diagram Owen seems to have exaggerated the difference between the two. Huxley immediately wrote to Owen, pointing out the error. When Owen replied, he blamed the artist. At one stage, Huxley accused Owen of mistranslating an account, originally in Dutch, of a chimpanzee's brain; however, according to some, the point that he made was irrelevant. At least some of the dispute hinged on problems of definition and the naming of different parts of the brain and was fairly petty. Huxley ended one particularly astringent letter to the *Athenaeum* by stating that he would 'hereafter deem it unnecessary to take cognizance of assertions, opposed to my own knowledge, to the concurrent testimony of all other original observers, and already publicly and formally refuted. Life is too short to occupy oneself with the slaying of the slain more than once.'[4]

Despite this statement, neither party would let the matter drop. At the annual meeting of the British Association, held in Cambridge in 1862, Thomas Huxley held the position of President of Section D, which was the section on 'Zoology and Botany, including Physiology': Owen presented two papers, both with an anti-Darwinian slant. The stage was set for confrontation. In a paper on 'The Zoological Significance of the Cerebral and Pedal Characters of Man', he compared the human brain and foot with those of the orangutans, chimpanzees and gorillas: he stressed the 'sudden advance' in the development of the brain, the 'marked hiatus between the highest grade of structure and the next step below'.

On the bones of the foot, he declaimed that although the bones of the toe were analogous, their disposition was different. (However, some might be tempted to see vague hints of evolutionary thinking in some of Owen's language – words such as 'gradation', 'advance' and 'step' can be found in his paper.)

Huxley attacked with vigour. A report in the *Athenaeum* opined that he 'appealed to the anatomists present . . . [to state that] the universal voice of Continental and British anatomists had not entirely born out [Huxley's] statements and refuted those of Prof. Owen'. Regarding the foot, Huxley asserted that the differences between humans and the apes were slight, a matter of degree, rather than in fundamentals. Some of the younger scientists in the audience supported Huxley with 'vehemence'. The antagonists failed to find common ground, Huxley and his disciples fighting about the details – the nature of the brain's posterior lobe, the posterior cornu and the hippocampus minor – rather than about the broader theme of Darwinian evolution. In later correspondence, Huxley used terms such as 'unworthy paltering with truth' and the 'untenability' of Owen's position. He probably overstated the situation. A careful reading of Owen's defence suggests that he never denied that the gorilla had a hippocampus minor; instead, he argued that it was not as well developed as in humans. In comparing humans with other animals, structures that were homologous, if unequal in size or development, might be given different names. There were also times when Owen, rather than uttering strong anti-evolutionary views, preferred to say that the mechanism by which new species were introduced to the living world was 'unknown'. In many of his popular lectures, a point of view not far from that of natural theology was apparent: the form of creatures ensured that they were adapted to their way of life, by dint of design on the part of the Creator. Structural similarities between organisms were seen as further arguments for intelligent design – that there had been a number of basic plans in the mind of the Creator.

Owen was always very conscious of his position: as we have seen, titles mattered to him. He had not been to Oxford or Cambridge, and his time as a student at Edinburgh was short. He had no title of Bachelor or Master of Arts (or, as in the case of some of his acquaintances, MD or DD). He had not attended Winchester College (as had William Buckland), or Westminster School (as had William Conybeare). He was very much a self-made man: in this, he resembled Huxley. After he was appointed to the Hunterian Professorship at the College of Surgeons, Owen greatly enjoyed lecturing or posing in his professorial gown, and he was frequently photographed wearing it. In the 1856 edition of the *London and Provincial Medical Directory*, he is described as the Hunterian Professor and Curator of the Museum of the Royal College of Surgeons of England.

Owen was evidently an excellent lecturer – he enjoyed being the centre of attention afforded by the podium – and he frequently gave popular lectures: perhaps this assisted in generating public support for his ideas for a new Museum of Natural History. He gave lectures to large audiences at the Museum of Practical Geology. He was also asked to lecture at the School of Mines as a visiting lecturer. However, here, several years before the Darwinian controversies, Owen came up against Thomas Huxley, who had been ensconced there for some time: Huxley had been a lecturer in natural history (which was taken to include palaeontology) for the School of Mines since 1854. When, in the 1857 version of the *Medical Directory*, Owen proclaimed himself to be a 'Professor of Comparative Anatomy and Palaeontology, Government School of Mines, Jermyn St', Huxley was incensed, and something of a scandal erupted. Sir Roderick Murchison, who held the combined posts of director-general of the Geological Survey, director of the School of Mines and of the Museum of Practical Geology, rebuked Owen, stating that he felt the title of Superintendent of the Natural History Collections at the British Museum overrode all others. This must have been somewhat humiliating for Owen: perhaps the incident contributed to the long-held antipathy between Huxley and Owen.

Several times, Huxley effectively declared himself the winner of the dispute with Owen – as in the letter published in the *Athenaeum*. In 1863, four years after *On the Origin of Species* was released, Huxley published a book entitled *Evidence as to Man's Place in Nature*, which included some material he had published previously at the time of the ongoing dispute with Owen. The book emphasizes the animal nature of humans and asserts that humanity could and should be studied in the context of its evolutionary history: humans and apes must have a common ancestor. The brain is extensively discussed, including the occurrence of the hippocampus minor in both apes and humans. In what Huxley hoped would be a final side-swipe at Owen, he declaimed:

> I now leave this subject, for the present. For the credit of my calling, I should be glad to be, hereafter, for ever silent upon it. But unfortunately, this is a matter upon which, after all that has occurred, no mistake or confusion of terms is possible – and, in affirming that the posterior lobe, the posterior cornu and the hippocampus minor, exist in certain Apes, I am stating either that which is true, or that which I know to be false. The question has thus become one of personal veracity. For myself, I will accept no other issue than this, grave as it is, to the personal controversy.

There were many who thought that this public brawling, particularly by Huxley, was undignified and inappropriate. For example, the medical journal *The Lancet* opined:

> We observe with regret that Mr Huxley has repeated his attack on Professor Owen, relative to the structures at the back part of the brain of man and apes. Anatomists and the [medical] profession became well aware, from Owen's reply to the first of these attacks, that the question was one of terms and definitions, not of facts . . . We recommend Professor Huxley to try to imitate . . . the calm and philosophical tone of the man whom he assails. The fling and the sneer, however smart, will only recoil upon himself.[5]

There had been times, of course, when Owen himself had been very free with the 'fling and the sneer'.

Darwin's *Descent of Man* entered the fray with a broadly similar message in 1871. There is an important link between this work by

Darwin and Huxley's *Man's Place*, for in some editions of *Descent* (for example, the second edition of 1874 and the popular reprints by John Murray, such as the 'New Edition' of 1906), an additional note has been included: the 'Note on the resemblances and differences in the structure and the development in man and apes. By Professor Huxley, FRS.' The opening of this short essay is worthy of quotation at some length:

> The controversy respecting the nature and extent of the differences in the structures of the brain in man and the apes, which arose fifteen years ago, has not yet come to an end . . . It was originally asserted and re-asserted, with singular pertinacity, that the brain of all the apes, even the highest, differs from that of man in the absence of such conspicuous structures as the posterior lobes of the cerebral hemispheres, with the cornu of the lateral ventricle and the hippocampus minor contained in those lobes which are so obvious in man . . . But the truth that the three structures in question are as well developed in the apes' as in human brains . . . stands at present on as secure support as any in comparative anatomy.

But Huxley's last word was more moderate. In his essay on Owen's contribution to comparative anatomy, in the Appendix to *The Life of Richard Owen* (1894), Huxley is, in places, quite gracious: perhaps he did not wish to speak ill of the dead. He admits that he is in a difficult position; there were 'many scientific controversies in which Owen was engaged'. However, after a review of the long history of anatomical science, at an early point in his analysis of Richard Owen's work, Huxley summarizes: 'During more than half a century, Owen's industry remained unabated; and whether we consider the quantity, or the quality, of the work done, or the wide range of his labours, I doubt if, in the long annals of anatomy, more is to be placed to the credit of a single worker.'

Huxley goes on to praise the 'five volumes of the descriptive catalogue of the Hunterian Museum, and of the annual courses of lectures demanded from the Hunterian Professor', which 'took

Owen over the length and breadth of the animal kingdom'. Huxley goes on to single out Owen's early work on the pearly nautilus, his study of the anatomy of the apes and monographs on the kiwi, the great auk and the dodo; he particularly admires Owen's work on fossil reptiles, and 'in 1863, the description of the famous reptilian bird, *Archaeopteryx*'. He continued, 'the historian of comparative anatomy, and of palaeontology, will always assign Owen a place next to, and hardly lower than, that of Cuvier, who was practically the creator of those sciences.' In terms of studying the forms of organisms, both extant and extinct, Huxley regarded Owen as almost without equal. 'But when we consider Owen's contributions to "philosophical anatomy", I think the epithet ceases to be appropriate,' Huxley writes, continuing:

> Thus, when Owen passes from matters of anatomical fact and their immediate interpretation to morphological speculation it is not surprising that he also passes from the camp of Cuvier into that of his adversaries . . . The explanation of the facts of morphology is sought in the 'principle of vegetative repetition'; in the interaction of a 'general and all-pervading polarising force', with an 'adaptive or special organising force'.[6]

Huxley almost ridiculed Owen's concepts of 'the archetype' and of 'secondary causes' for the 'progression of natural phenomena'; he decried Owen's flirtation with 'realistic mysticism' and 'sublimated theism'. Huxley concludes by noting that although there were 'wide differences of opinion which unhappily obtained between Sir R. Owen and myself', Owen had made 'great and solid achievements in Comparative Anatomy and Palaeontology' and his 'high place among those who have made great and permanently valuable contributions to knowledge remain[s] unassailable'.

7

The Evolution of Owen's Evolutionary Ideas

When Richard Owen embarked on his career in comparative anatomy, on his appointment to the curatorship at the Hunterian Collection at the Royal College of Surgeons in 1826, and particularly when he was appointed lecturer in comparative anatomy at St Bartholomew's Hospital a few months later, it was assumed that the comparison of the anatomy of different organisms with one another, and with humans, was a worthwhile endeavour. However, it was only a relatively short time previously that the groundwork for this could first have been said to be performed.

The foundations of the subject were securely laid on the continent. Johann Friedrich Blumenbach began teaching a course on the subject at Göttingen in 1785, publishing his *Handbuch der Vergleichenden Anatomie* (Handbook of Comparative Anatomy) a few years later; another academic at the University of Leipzig, Carl Gustav Carus, published his *Lehrbuch der Zootomie*, or textbook of zootomy (zootomy being defined as the 'dissection or anatomy of animals'). Perhaps the greatest continental exponent in the field, however, was Cuvier. He was also a pioneer of stratigraphy (the branch of geology concerned with the relative order and positions of rock strata, together with their relationship to the geological timescale). Cuvier believed that the different parts of a creature's anatomy functioned as an integrated whole: if an animal had a carnivore's teeth, then its whole anatomy would reflect the anatomy of a carnivorous organism: form was related to function. He showed the striking similarity of the Indian elephant to the extinct fossil mammoth, thereby displaying an understanding of the phenomenon of extinction. Cuvier gained a reputation for being able to reconstruct an extinct creature from a few fossil fragments – a skill that Owen later prided himself upon sharing. Owen claimed that he was able to do this, treating organisms as fixed and integrated wholes, in which every characteristic had a fixed value that was set by all the other characteristics.

Cuvier also believed that the Earth was of relatively recent origin, yet he argued that there had existed a 'world previous to ours'. In fact, he believed that there had been a series of stages, represented by the various layers of rock in the Paris basin, each inhabited by its distinctive assemblage of animals (fossils) that had been rendered extinct by some catastrophe. He considered the Great Flood, which is described in the Book of Genesis, to be perhaps the last of these catastrophic events.[1] Cuvier was strongly opposed to any evolutionary ideas.

In 1831 Richard Owen spent a few weeks in Paris and witnessed the tail-end of the 'great debates' between Cuvier and Étienne Geoffroy Saint-Hilaire. Geoffroy expanded and defended Lamarck's evolutionary theories, although his scientific views had a more transcendental tone (in contrast to Lamarck's more materialistic views) and were similar to those of German morphologists, such as Lorenz Oken (1779–1851). He believed in the underlying unity of organism design and the possibility of the transmutation of species over time, amassing evidence for his claims through his research in comparative anatomy, embryology and palaeontology. It should be remembered here that there were strong political undercurrents to the biological debate: Geoffroy was anti-royalist, while the somewhat autocratic Cuvier supported the monarchy. The two men disagreed about many matters other than science.

The naturalists of the late eighteenth century, such as Linnaeus, emphasized the *form* of organisms and utilized the appearance and structure of plants and animals as a guide to their classification. Their emphasis was on observation and rigorous description. The thinking of these naturalists reflected the era of the Enlightenment and its emphasis on the study of the material world and, likewise, on rationalism.

Ambroise Tardieu, *Étienne Geoffroy Saint-Hilaire*, c. 1823, engraving.

In the earlier decades of the nineteenth century, there was something of a movement away from this mechanistic approach to natural history; it was at this point that a Romantic philosophy of nature developed.

One of the precepts of this approach was the notion of unity in diversity. There exist similarities in form that bind together, in some rather mysterious way, the immense variety of organic forms. All flowering plants have a certain similarity in their structure. All vertebrates, despite their enormous variety – birds, mammals, amphibians, reptiles and even fish – can be envisaged as having a basic architectural plan. Transcendental anatomy is the notion that all living beings, despite their great variety and complexity, can be seen as belonging to a relatively small number of basic forms. Some even believed that the mineral world could be brought into this conspectus.

A related idea that was emphasized by some naturalists of the transcendental anatomy school was that of the Chain of Being: the idea that minerals, plants and animals can be arranged in a series of increasing complexity. Some, indeed, saw higher forms as recapitulating those forms lower in the scheme. Others tried to arrange all natural forms into a three-dimensional, branching system.

A particular manifestation of the recapitulation doctrine is the idea that the embryological development of an organism – its *ontology* – reflects the pattern of development of the series of creatures that gave rise to it. Among the exponents of these recapitulatory ideas were Lorenz Oken and J. F. Meckel (1781–1833), as well as Étienne Geoffroy Saint-Hilaire. Richard Owen had seen the last of these in action in Paris in 1830, when in a debate with Georges Cuvier.

In the early years of Owen's scientific career, there were still many naturalists who could be considered comparative anatomists, on the continent at least; moreover, they had developed a number of conceptual frameworks to explain the perceived similarities that they found. Some of these transcendental theories had a vaguely evolutionary character.

It was Owen's ambition to become known as the leading exponent of comparative anatomy in Europe and to attain a position that rivalled, or even exceeded, that of Cuvier and his German colleague Meckel. In a letter to his friend the naturalist and cleric Professor Buckland of Christ Church, Oxford, in 1842, Owen expressed his aspiration of writing the definitive 'general treatise on Comparative Anatomy, with the requisite illustrations'. Fiercely nationalistic as he was, Owen continued:

I am unwilling that England should lose the credit of producing that work on Comparative Anatomy, which France and Germany have, as yet, failed in achieving . . . I indulge in no less hopes that the completion of such a survey of the highest class of created things on this planet as will be recognized to be parallel [with] that which Cuvier and Meckel have attempted to give.[2]

The whole point of studying comparative anatomy was surely to show the similarities (and differences) between organisms, and, where possible, to explain them. Owen set about this task with vigour.

One of the reasons underpinning Richard Owen's undoubted success was the wide range of scales at which he worked. Early in his career, he took 'a considerable interest in microscopical work'. In his biography of his grandfather, Richard Owen Jr reported:

[He] had made many observations in the corpuscles of the blood in man and other animals. At this time [1839], Dr J. E. Bowerbank, of Highgate, gathered around him a few friends . . . for the discussion of microscopical problems. This little band used to meet at each other's homes. Eventually Bowerbank . . . and the rest determined to form a society which should have for its object microscopical research. Owen, from his abilities and position, was selected as the first president of the new society, and he occupied the chair in 1840 and 1841, and delivered the first two presidential addresses of the Royal Microscopical Society.[3]

Richard Owen therefore worked at the microscopic level, at the level of organs (such as bones, teeth, the heart or the brain), at the level of biological systems or 'organization' and the level of the whole organism. However, the ecological approach, the study of organisms relative to their environment and habitat, was perhaps lacking.

During the first meeting of the Microscopical Society, Owen showed the applicability of the microscope to the study of teeth, and in particular to the teeth of fossil organisms. He compared both the microscopic and macroscopic features of the teeth of a wide range of animals in his two-volume work *Odontography* (1840–45), which was subtitled *A Treatise on the Comparative Anatomy of the Teeth: Their Physiological Relations, Mode of Development and Microscopic Structure in the Vertebrate Animals*. This work was also partly derived from his Hunterian lectures. Somewhat later, he felt able to write about the science of comparative anatomy:

A very important application of comparative anatomy is the determination of the degrees of complexity in the organisation of different animals, and the number and value of points of resemblance which different species manifest to each other and in the totality of their organisation. A study of the anatomy of animals, guided by these views, is essential to the determination of their natural affinities, which is the highest aim of the philosophic naturalist.[4]

A dissection of this paragraph would emphasize the following points:

– The study of comparative anatomy should be directed at comparing the organization of organisms.
– Organisms vary particularly in their degree of complexity.
– Species differ from each other by different amounts, and it is possible to estimate the 'value' of the 'points of resemblance'.
– From noting these similarities and differences, the 'natural affinities' of organisms may be discerned.

The reader will have noted that this analysis appears to be but a step away from an evolutionary position. However, immediately following the paragraph quoted above, there appears the following statement:

Lastly, the labours of comparative anatomists continually tend to bring to light examples of structures designed with reference to especial purposes, of the most striking and forcible description: and thus provide for the moralist and divine a storehouse of facts peculiarly adapted to the illustration of the doctrine of final causes.

Aristotle expounded the idea of the 'final cause', maintaining that all objects, including those of nature, had a purpose, ultimate objective or *telos* (τέλος). Teleology, therefore, is the explanation of phenomena in the real world in terms of the purpose they serve

Unknown artist, *John Ray*, *c.* 1685–90, oil on canvas.

rather than of the manner in which they arise. In theology, it is the doctrine of design and purpose in the material world, following the ideas expounded by John Ray (1691) and William Paley (1810).[5] Here, Owen is not so much making a statement in favour of, or against, evolutionary ideas, but instead maintaining that the investigation of the role that structure – whether macroscopic or microscopic – plays in the organism's life, or the relationship of form to function, is more important than considering a phenomenon's origin.

At around about the same time, Owen published some of the other material from the Hunterian lectures that he had been giving

at the College of Surgeons: *Lectures on the Comparative Anatomy
. . . of Invertebrate Animals*, which appeared in 1843, and a
companion, *Vertebrate Animals*, which appeared in 1846 (the
latter dealing only with fishes). With these publications, Owen
was proclaiming that comparative anatomy was fully established
in England, as well as giving the prestigious Hunterian lectures,
the Collection, and his role in them the appropriate publicity.
When compared to Cuvier, Owen always asserted that he had his
own approach. While he respected the work of his continental
colleagues, he was not greatly in awe of them.

Nevertheless, the debt of science to continental natural history
in the years 1830–45 – the very years comprising the first part
of Owen's scientific career – was substantial. Its influence on
comparative anatomy, palaeontology (particularly vertebrate
palaeontology) and embryology was particularly noticeable. One
factor here was the impact of transcendentalism, the search for an
underlying unity, and the use of clear conceptual frameworks for the
arrangement of observations.

In 1846, under the auspices of the British Association for the
Advancement of Science (BAAS), Richard Owen published a work
with which his name will always be associated: *The Report on the
Archetype and Homologies of the Vertebrate Skeleton*. He produced
several other publications of a similar character and with broadly
similar objectives: for example, 'Teleology of the Skeleton of Fishes',
in the *Edinburgh New Philosophical Journal* in 1847. Another book,
published in 1848, repeated some of the material found in the BAAS
Report.

Owen was concerned to show that there were a limited number
of basic forms, or 'designs', among organisms. For each group of
organisms, a basic or ideal form existed, and a number of variations
could be identified. An 'archetype' was the basic pattern to which
all the creatures in a particular group (such as the vertebrates)
conformed.

Thus 'homologies' or 'homologues' can be discerned. A
'homologue' was defined by Owen as 'the same organ in different
animals under every variety of form and function', distinguishing

this from an 'analogue', which was 'a part or organ of one animal which has the same function as another part or organ in a different animal'. Thus homologues may often be analogues, although the reverse is not always the case. The pectoral fin of a porpoise is homologous with that of a fish: it is also analogous. On the other hand, the wing or the parachute of the little *Draco volans* – the flying lizard of Southeast Asia – is analogous to the wing of a bird or of a bat but is not homologous with it. In both cases, the organ in question is used for flying (or at least gliding from tree to tree, in the lizard's case), but the wing of a bird (or bat) is a modified forelimb, while that of the lizard is a lateral extension of the skin of the thorax.

The archetype of the vertebrates, according to Owen, was an elongate creature, consisting of a series of similar segments – a type of homology in itself – each of which he called a vertebra: in living (and fossil) vertebrates, some of these are fused to form the skull and others the tail, whereas still more are modified in other ways.

The skeletons of mammals, birds, fish, reptiles and amphibians all conform to this model or archetype; 'the extent to which . . . the organisation of a specific animal' deviates from its archetype 'becomes an index of the grade of each species' and speaks directly to its 'ascent in the scale of being'. Even in man, the lineaments of the broad pattern of the archetype could be discerned.

Owen thus demonstrated, with great clarity, that all vertebrates were constructed according to a basic plan. His publications on the subject were extraordinarily detailed, giving examples from many different organisms. Moreover, the extent to which their form represents an elaboration of this basic plan provides an indication of its position 'on the scale of being'. In using the prefix 'arch' in the term 'archetype', Owen was thinking in terms of the word-element derived from the ancient Greek, ἀρχός (*arkhós*), meaning 'ruler'; or ἀρχικός (*arkhikós*), meaning 'ruling'. The archetype was envisaged as an idea, a conceptual framework or a design template in the mind of the Creator, some sort of divine forethought that ruled or dominated the process of Creation. A predetermined pattern existed. Individual species, however, were adapted to their environment and way of life, as part of the divine plan.

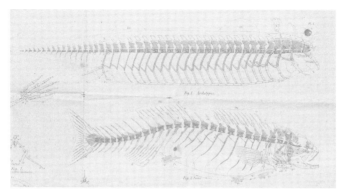

Richard Owen's archetype skeleton compared with that of a fish, from *On the Nature of Limbs* (1849).

Owen followed the analysis of homologies shown by the vertebrate skeleton with a study, 'On the Homologies and Notation of the Dental System of Mammalia', and a paper, 'On the Value of Nerves as a Homological Character'. A book called *On the Nature of Limbs* applied a similar approach: the wings of birds and bats, the legs of mammals, birds and amphibians, and the fins of cetaceans (whales, porpoises and dolphins) – all had a similar basic bone structure, although the details of the limbs' forms were reflective of the particular organism's lifestyle and environment. The understanding that creatures were adapted to their habitat was already widely accepted.

Much of this work was well received by the naturalists and other scientists of the time: in particular, the high level of detail provided in the comparison of the skeletons of a wide range of vertebrates was appreciated. However, Richard Owen ended his 1846 BAAS paper as follows:

With regard to the 'adaptive force', whatever may be the expressions by which its nature and relations, when better understood, may be attempted to be explained, its effects must ever impress the rightly constituted mind [with] the conviction that in every species, 'ends are obtained, and the interests of the animal promoted, in a way that indicates superior design, intelligence and foresight; but a design, intelligence and foresight in which the judgement and reflection of the animal never were concerned; and which, therefore, with Virgil, and with other studious observers of nature, we must ascribe to the Sovereign of the universe in which we live, move and have our being.'[6]

The long sentences, the sometimes rather obscure meaning, the vagueness and the occasional reference to classical authors were not atypical of Owen's style. These, together with the lapses into metaphysical thought, did not appeal to all his readers.

Elsewhere, Owen wrote of an 'organising force' that produces the structure of the archetype, suggesting that it is akin to the forces that cause crystallization and the adoption of a crystalline structure. When writing about the king crab (*Limulus polyphemus*) and its relationship to its ancient predecessors in the fossil record, he declaimed that there must exist a 'preordained plan of derivation by congenital departures from the parental form'. He also referred vaguely to a 'secondary cause or law'. Yet other phrases that he used included the 'vital principle', and 'ordained continuous becoming'.

The vague notions of a 'preordained plan' and an 'organising force' increasingly isolated Owen from his peers. Such metaphysical imponderables were anathema to some philosophers and naturalists.

For example, the critic, philosopher and amateur physiologist G. H. Lewes (1817–1878) wrote:

Metaphysical ghosts cannot be killed, because they cannot be touched; but they may be dispelled by dispelling the twilight in which shadows and solidities are easily confounded. The Vital Principle is an entity of this ghostly kind; and although the daylight has dissipated it, and positive Biology is no longer vexed with its visitations, it nevertheless reappears in another shape in the shadowy region of mystery which surrounds biological and all other questions.[7]

As has been shown, evolutionary ideas were very much in the air before Charles Darwin's *On the Origin of Species* was published in 1859. Therefore, by the early 1860s, Owen's archetype and his notions of an 'adaptive force' and so on would no longer be accepted. To take a single example, an anonymous author, not altogether dismissive of Owen's views, declaimed in the *Medical Times and Gazette* in January 1863:

> We prefer to believe that the archetypical vertebrate skeleton, whatever exact form it might have possessed, was once manifested in the flesh as an objective entity, than conceive it merely as a process of the Creator's thought . . . [I]nductive students seeking in the vast field of osteological science a *vera causa* for the relations which animals admittedly bear to some common type, from the assemblage of corroborative facts before them, will accept the corollary of the existence of an original supreme archetypical pattern of life, whence all forms have been derived, either by successive creation, through the fiat of the Almighty Life-giver, or by descent, with modification operating through laws analogous to those which govern the reproduction and succession of individuals.[8]

The anonymous author, who could be criticized for his remarkably lugubrious style (not totally dissimilar to that of Owen), could also be accused of having covered his bet both ways. Nevertheless, he raises the possibility of the archetype being some early and original form, from which the subsequent diversity of beings was derived by descent, in accordance with ascertainable, natural laws or processes. From this, it follows that throughout time, there had been a succession of forms, as well as a succession of individuals.

Darwin himself, although he quotes Owen, in some cases respectfully, in *On the Origin,* was certainly well aware that Owen's work in comparative anatomy provided powerful support for his theory. The following passage, from the last chapter of *On the Origin,* is a clear acknowledgement of the value of Owen's work comparing the skeletons of vertebrates:

The framework of bones being the same in the hand of man, wing of a bat, fin of a porpoise, and leg of a horse, – the same number of vertebrae forming the neck of the giraffe and of the elephant, – and innumerable other such facts, at once explain themselves on the theory of descent with slow and slight modifications. The similarity of pattern in the wing and leg of a bat, though used for such different purposes . . . is likewise intelligible on the view of the gradual modification of parts or organs which were alike in the early progenitor.

The archetype had become the ancestor. Owen's work on archetypes fed into Darwinian evolution perfectly.

To what extent was Owen a transmutationist? It does seem, at certain times in his career, that he was more sympathetic to evolutionary ideas than at others. For example, towards the end of *On the Nature of Limbs* (1849), a work that emphasizes the ideas of archetype and homologue, there does appear the somewhat veiled suggestion that humans were derived from lower forms of life as the result of natural laws,

such terms also indicating, *obscurely indeed*, so much perception of the pre-existing model as could be obtained from the study of one form, at a period when that form – the human frame – [in the past] was viewed as something not only above, but distinct from, if not antithetical to the structures of brute creation, and . . . it was little suspected that all the parts and origins of man had been sketched out, in anticipation, so to speak, in the inferior animals.[9] (Emphasis added)

A comment in the *Manchester Spectator* rebuked the author for denying the role of the Almighty in creating humans. Owen may have backed away from such transmutationist thinking, recalling the criticisms that were thrown at evolutionary ideas in Chambers's *Vestiges of the Natural History of Creation* (originally published anonymously) in 1844, just a few years before. The author of *Vestiges* had been heavily criticized. Owen, always extremely conscious of his position in society, had to be careful.

Perhaps this was the reason for his indirect style. However, some critics, attempting to penetrate Owen's wordy prose, interpreted this passage as stating that humans evolved from fish, thus denying that all creatures, including humans, were created by God. One is tempted to believe that, sometimes, Owen deliberately obfuscated. Phrases such as 'opaquely written' have, on occasion, been used to describe some of Owen's books and papers.

Although his writing is often vague and convoluted, from about the later 1840s onwards Owen does seem to have accepted the possibility of some form of evolution, by means of what he called 'secondary mechanisms'. He seems to have thought in terms of several possible mechanisms for some sort of evolutionary process:

Parthenogenesis. In 1745, it was shown that some aphids – or plant lice – were capable of reproducing without sexual union: several asexual generations can be born before a generation in which sexual reproduction occurs. Subsequently, the phenomenon was described in other organisms. In 1849 Owen discussed the topic in his Hunterian lecture series, in which he, unsuccessfully, attempted to explain the phenomenon. Later, he wrote that: 'The first acquaintance of these marvels excited the hope that we are about to penetrate the mystery of the origin of different species of animals but, as far as observation has yet extended, the cycle is definitely closed.'[10]

Prolonged development. Many organisms, such as insects, undergo a metamorphosis: from egg to larva, pupa and imago. In some cases, there are even more stages, all of which, if found in isolation, might be regarded as separate species. If, occasionally, a further stage in development were to occur, this might provide a mechanism for the bringing into existence of a new species. At some stages of his career, Owen attempted to show that the extinct forms of an organism represented more general structures, while the later forms represented more specialized examples. He suggested that the embryonic forms through which a creature passes represent earlier, extinct members of its class.

Premature development. Analogously, the embryos of animals undergo stages of development. The early stages in the development of a vertebrate, for example, look very different from the 'full-term' youngster. Should an immature creature gain the ability to reproduce, it could be argued that a new species might eventuate. This notion has been given credibility by research on the axolotl (*Ambystoma mexicanum*), a species of salamander that is nearly extinct in its native Mexico, which reaches sexual maturity while still in the larval, 'tadpole', gill-bearing stage (neoteny). When given certain hormone injections, it has been proved that it is possible to make these axolotls complete their metamorphosis. In their final state, they closely resemble adult salamanders of a related species.

Lamarckian hypertrophy. Richard Owen visited France and met many French naturalists in 1830, at a time when the memory of Jean-Baptiste Lamarck (1744–1829) must have still been respected; Owen was quite familiar with some of Lamarck's ideas, although he was not uncritical of them. One of Lamarck's 'laws' was that in the case of an animal that has not passed the limit of its development, the frequent and continuous use of a particular organ tends to strengthen, develop and enlarge that organ, giving it a power proportional to the amount of time it has been so used. Moreover, Lamarck suggested, such characteristics could be inherited.

Lamarckian atrophy. This is the opposite of the above circumstances. Lamarck asserted that the long-term disuse of an organ tended to cause it to become weak and deteriorate. Thus it is progressively diminished in its functional capacity, and may ultimately disappear. Owen adopted a concept somewhat close to this in his discussion of the dodo.

Congenital malformations. These are physical defects that are

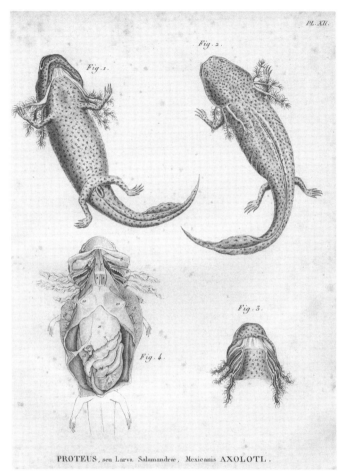

The Axolotl (*Ambystoma mexicanum*), a Mexican salamander that can reproduce in its larval form, from Alexander von Humboldt, *Beobachtungen aus der Zoologie und vergleichenden Anatomie* (1806).

present in a young organism at birth, sometimes involving many different parts of the body. Congenital malformations can be genetic and are thus heritable; they can also result from exposing the foetus to a malformation agent (in humans, for example, due to the mother drinking alcohol or smoking), or they can be of unknown origin.

It was full-blown 'transmutation' as an idea, and later the doctrine of natural selection as a mechanism for evolution, that Owen opposed. Maybe it was the individual who originated the idea, as much as the notion itself, that Owen detested. Darwin certainly thought it was jealousy over the success of *On the Origin* that contributed to Richard Owen's rancour. (Earlier, as we have seen, Owen had dreamt of becoming the supreme authority in England on comparative anatomy, and the ascendancy of Darwin, even though he was in no sense a real competitor, infuriated him.) Often Owen's arguments and language were anything but straightforward: as late as 1860, he was referring to the *Apteryx* (kiwi) of New Zealand and the red grouse of England as 'separate creations'. Time and again, Owen used expressions such as 'Divine Power' but also the 'ordained becoming' of living things.

In any event, when preparing the first edition of *On the Origin*, Darwin assumed that Richard Owen was opposed to evolutionary theories. In the final paragraph of Chapter Nine, 'Imperfections in the Geological Record', Darwin admitted the rarity of transitional forms in the geological record, and included Owen's name among those palaeontologists who argued strongly that species were immutable. Some scholars have maintained that it was this denial that Owen accepted *any* change in a species over time that incurred his anger against Darwin. Bearing in mind the obscurantist language that Owen used, Darwin could be forgiven for this assumption. By the later 1860s, Owen came close to maintaining that natural selection was his own idea. Perhaps he was justified when he claimed to have 'anticipated' the notion, but he never fully embraced it.

In his early years at the College of Surgeons, Owen was charged with editing some of John Hunter's manuscripts and, in one of the essays, the question is asked: 'Does not the natural gradation of animals from one to another lead to the original species?' Different varieties of the dog lead back to the wolf, he argued. Similar gradations could be seen in the horse, sheep and cat. Darwin argued along the same lines. Owen had enormous respect for Hunter's work, and one is tempted to wonder whether these fragmentary ideas, which were never fully expanded by Hunter, could have had some influence on Owen.

In some of his earlier publications, Owen used the term 'centres of creation'. Darwin also used the term, for example, in some of his notebooks that he kept on the *Beagle* voyage, from 1831 to 1836.

In later editions of *On the Origin*, from 1861 onwards, Darwin included a 'sketch' tracing the development of evolutionary ideas, which paid some acknowledgement to the complexity of Owen's position. It is perhaps worth quoting Darwin's words more fully:

When the first edition of this work was published, I was completely deceived, as were many others, by such expressions as 'the continuous operation of creative power' that I included Professor Owen with other palaeontologists as being firmly convinced of the immutability of species; but it appears that this on my part was a preposterous error. In the last edition of this work I inferred, and the inference still seems perfectly just . . . that Professor Owen admitted that natural selection may have done something in the formation of new species; but this, it appears, is inaccurate. I also gave some extracts from a correspondence between Professor Owen and the editor of the 'London Review', from which it appeared manifest to the editor, as well as to myself, that Professor Owen claimed to have promulgated the theory of natural selection before I had done so; and I expressed my surprise and satisfaction at this announcement; but as far as it is possible to understand certain recently published passages, I have again fallen into error. It is consolatory to me that others find Professor Owen's controversial writings as difficult to understand and to reconcile with each other as I do.

Does one not detect a note of patient exasperation in Darwin's tone?

There are hints in some of his later work, albeit sometimes vague, that Owen was increasingly close to an evolutionary position. A paper he gave to the Geological Society in 1878 (when he was 73) was titled 'On the Influence of the Advent of a Higher Form in Modifying the Structure of an Older and Lower Form'; its very title surely implies the acceptance of some part of the theory of evolution. It also shows a remarkable ecological awareness, to appreciate that the advent of a new organism in an ecosystem could occasion changes in others that are already present. The particular example that Owen had in mind was the appearance of mammals in the Tertiary period that affected the structure of the skull of crocodiles. As these 'large mammalian quadrupeds' came more frequently to drink on the banks of water-bodies, the crocodiles' methods of feeding changed from a fish diet to one including the higher vertebrates: the position of the nostrils altered in some later Crocodilia species, along with other changes in the jaws and skull, as well as in their limbs. When challenged about this, Owen stressed that he was referring to adaptation rather than evolution; in any case, he tended towards a Lamarckian mechanism rather than one involving natural selection.[11]

Towards the very end of his career, when he was in his late seventies, and after Darwin's death, Richard Owen's hubris seems to have dissipated. In 1882, he wrote an appreciation of his erstwhile adversary:

> The great value of Darwin's series of works, summarising all the evidences of embryology, palaeontology and physiology, experimentally applied to producing varieties of species is exemplified in the general acceptance by biologists of the secondary law, by evolution, of the 'origin of species'. As a rule . . . monographs now published in natural history are in terms of such a 'law'.[12]

It has already been hinted that, throughout a good deal of his career, Sir Richard Owen, as he eventually became, strove to be on good terms, as far as was possible, with 'establishment' figures – Oxbridge clergy, parliamentarians, aristocrats and similar worthies. Just possibly, one who had taught the Royal children and been on committees with Queen Victoria's consort, whatever his innermost thoughts, would not want to come down too firmly and heavily on the side of what was, at the time, the very progressive and controversial idea of evolution through natural selection.

8

Museums and Committees

From the earliest days of his career, Richard Owen was a museum man. The idea of fieldwork – of studying living organisms in their natural environment – was almost anathema to him. Nor did he attach much importance to the behaviour of animals. In both of these attitudes, he was very different from Darwin; since his teenage years, Darwin collected beetles in the woods and fields of Shropshire, and throughout his days on HMS *Beagle*, he recorded the behaviour, gait and sounds of the creatures he encountered, often showing an understanding of how creatures related to their environment or habitat. In Owen's world, mammals, birds, fish and reptiles were to be studied once dead, as museum specimens or on the dissection table. The opening sentence of his first major publication – *Memoir on the Pearly Nautilus* – runs, 'The true relations of every class of animal are now acknowledged to depend for their development on anatomical investigation.'

The account of his life, written by his grandson, is recorded as follows:

On August 18, 1826, Owen obtained his membership of the Royal College of Surgeons. His diploma is signed by John Abernethy [among others] . . . Owen's peculiar ability as a dissector had not escaped Abernethy, then President of the College of Surgeons, who, much concerned at the neglect of the collections formed by John Hunter, which had recently been purchased by the Government and handed over to the care of the College, insisted on his old pupil undertaking their arrangement . . . When first appointed, Owen found at the museum no adequate catalogue of any department, either manuscript or printed . . . Owen's first difficult task, therefore, was to prepare a descriptive catalogue of the collection.[1]

And what a collection it was. The surgical pioneer John Hunter had of course accumulated medical and surgical specimens, but there were also specimens that had been collected by Joseph Banks 'during the circumnavigatory voyage of Captain Cook'. Parts I to VI of the catalogue, which were partly the work of Richard Owen, but under the supervision of William Clift, the curator, appeared in 1830 and 1831.[2] Part IV(i) was apparently entirely Owen's work. There were around 13,700 specimens to be examined and described, and, as most of the original documents relating to the material had been lost or destroyed (according to some sources, deliberately) by a predecessor, Owen had to examine fresh specimens in a number of cases. A further set of illustrated catalogues of the 'Physiological series of comparative anatomy in the Museum of the Royal College of Surgeons' appeared between 1832 and 1835; 'Organs of motion and digestion' appeared in volume I, while those of the 'circulating, respiratory and urinary systems' appeared in volume II of this series, and so on. Yet another set of catalogues, listing 'fossil organic remains', appeared between 1845 and 1856. The task of describing the collections and compiling these catalogues has been described as a 'Herculean labour'.

Owen strove to ensure that the museums for which he had responsibility – first the Hunterian Collection, later, the natural history department of the British Museum, later still the independent British Museum (Natural History) – were a credit to Britain. He frequently compared British science, and British museums, with those of continental nations. In 1831, after having paid a visit to Paris and being impressed by French efforts in this direction, he compiled a 'Report on the Muséum d'Anatomie Comparée'. It had long been his ambition to establish the Hunterian Collection as a museum of international standing in the field of comparative anatomy.

Thomas H. Shepherd, *Hunterian Museum, Royal College of Surgeons, London*, 1828, engraving.

Owen, through his connections at the Zoological Society, also had the right of first refusal to dissect any creature that had died at the zoo (which could be considered a particular kind of museum) and to publish his findings in the *Proceedings* of the Society. By the end of 1832, when he was just 28, he had published 27 papers on the anatomy of different species of mammals, birds and invertebrates, using the resources of the zoo and the museum (this total output did not include the several parts of the catalogue).

The assistant curatorship of the Hunterian Museum to some extent acted as a springboard for Owen's career. Very shortly after taking up the position, he was able to combine it with a lectureship at St Bartholomew's Hospital, upgraded to a Chair (Professorship) in 1834. Upon William Clift's retirement, he took over as conservator of the Hunterian Museum in 1842. In 1837 he was also appointed to a professorship at what was by then the Royal College of Surgeons, a Royal Charter being bestowed on it in 1800. As part of his duties, he was to give a series of lectures – the Hunterian lectures – every year, from 1837 to 1855. These lectures – three one-hour lectures per week, given in March, April and May – were firmly based on his work at the Hunterian Museum. The titles of some of the series of Owen's orations reflected those of the catalogue titles. Thus a synergy developed between Owen's curatorial work, his advocacy on the importance of the collections, his lectures and his publications. In a Hunterian lecture in 1842, he declaimed:

> Collections of natural objects, selected for their significance, rarity or beauty have ever been regarded as the signs and ornaments of civilised nations: and though at first viewed with feelings of curiosity and wonder, they soon become recognised as important aids to the acquisition of intellectual wealth.

Here, as throughout his life, Richard Owen, who had seen the Jardin des Plantes and associated collections in Paris, was losing no opportunity to emphasize the role of great museums and collections for the 'intellectual wealth', and hence the prestige, of a nation.

It was a theme to which he frequently returned. To take one other example from a lecture he gave to the Royal Institution in April 1861, he took it as self-evident that museums were something to be encouraged: 'I may assume the general admission that collections of the several classes of objects, duly prepared, named, and arranged, so as to give the utmost facility for inspection and comparison, are the indispensable instruments in the acquisition and advance of . . . knowledge.'[3] A little later in the same lecture, he again linked the display of unique natural history specimens with national prestige: 'St Petersburg justly boasts the stuffed skin of its unique Mammoth: Madrid was as famous for its once unique Magatherium.'

Although in the years prior to Richard Owen's appointment at the Royal College of Surgeons, Hunterian lectures had been on the techniques of surgery and practical medical matters, Owen, with the full support of the college, took a different approach, emphasizing comparative anatomy. For example, in 1841, he spoke on 'The comparative anatomy of the generative organs and the development of the ovum and foetus in different classes of animals'; in the following year, the topic was 'Comparative and fossil osteology'. Although medical students attended in some numbers, along with numerous London medical men, Owen's lectures attracted a wider audience of at times as many as eight hundred people. Attending became something of a 'society activity'; representatives of the aristocracy, the clergy and the scientific elite were to be seen attending such events. William Buckland, of Christ Church, Oxford, Thomas Carlyle, the 'Sage of Chelsea', and Samuel Wilberforce were sometimes to be seen in the audience. All this was exactly as Richard Owen wished, expanding the reputation of the museum and of course himself. The esteem in which the lectures were held was partly the result of Owen's reputation for being *scientific*. Even with the college's Royal Charter, the reputation of the medical and surgical professions still left something to be desired, and the bloodiness of surgery revolted many; the separation of the barbers from the surgeons, formerly grouped together as the Company of Barber-Surgeons, which had existed in London since medieval times, had only occurred in 1745, less than a century previously. It was not until the passage of the Medical Act of 1858 that some consistency was put into medical training. 'Physic' and surgery were still sometimes considered trades that were entered via apprenticeship (as, initially, was the case with Owen), rather than professions for which practitioners became qualified through rigorous academic training. A little scientific rigour did the college no harm. One student of Hunter declared that the lectures were intended: 'To keep alive the public-minded exertions of Mr Hunter [and by implication the reputation of the museum that housed his collections], to cherish and encourage those abstract researches which give the Healing Art a claim to be associated with the Sciences.'⁴ Just as the lectures were sometimes indebted to the museum catalogues, so some of Richard Owen's papers were sometimes based on the lectures. Again, we see something of a symbiosis between his museum work, his lecturing and his publications.

Fossil organisms were well represented in the Hunterian Collection, and papers on palaeontology were authored by Owen from 1833 onwards. The Hunterian lectures for 1855, for example, were entitled, 'On the structure and habits of extinct vertebrate animals, illustrated by the Hunterian series of fossil remains'. Some 3,709 of the more than 13,700 specimens in the collection were fossils, and Darwin had entrusted the description of the fossil vertebrates that he brought back from South America to Owen. The 1839 incident, in which Richard Owen deduced the former existence of the giant, flightless bird, the moa or *Diornis*, as recounted in Chapter Three, is testament to both the collection's and Owen's importance to palaeontology; in the *Report on British Fossil Reptiles* (1842 and 1844), which was so well-received by the British Association, Owen was the one to coin the term 'dinosaur'.

This commitment to palaeontology, together with other areas of 'pure science', did not go unquestioned. There were those who believed strongly that the first duty and function of the Royal College of Surgeons was to advance surgery. In reviewing one of Owen's palaeontological works, 'Description of the Skeleton of an Extinct Gigantic Sloth (*Mylodon robustus*) . . .', which had been published (and funded) by the Royal College, the medical journal *The Lancet* sarcastically commented on the 'splendid tome' that had been published 'for the advancement of practical surgery, and the knowledge and treatment of those diseases and accidents to which the human frame is liable, and which are taken by the College of Surgeons under its special care.'[5]

More transparently, the review also remarked on the work's

> utter worthlessness to the surgeons of Great Britain – to the men by whose contributions this College is entirely supported . . . [I]t can only be regarded by all conscientious men who have any concern in the matter, as a profligate expenditure of the funds of its members, and a palpable misoccupation of the time and talents of their servant, the curator.

Unease grew within the college itself. Was the funding of research and the publication of works in comparative anatomy and palaeontology – such as monographs on the pearly nautilus and the extinct giant sloth – the best use of the college's resources? Owen had long since given up the practice of surgery himself, but there may have been other reasons why he was never elevated to the council of the college.

For there were, indeed, numerous other difficulties; Owen thought that his salary was insufficient in relation to his scientific status and his responsibilities, particularly in comparison with those who were on the council of the college and the trustees of the collection. These bodies tended to be self-perpetuating, and some of the members rarely, if ever, attended meetings. There were times when these bodies actually sought to reduce his salary. There were criticisms of his work, which Owen thought were unfair, and embedded calumnies – some of them in print. There were suggestions that he was spending too much time on his lecturing and on research, rather than on the preparation of catalogues, which was the primary task for which he was appointed. The council prevented him from accepting other work and honours; for example, in 1837, Owen was offered the prestigious Fullerton professorship at the Royal Institution, but he was forced to decline. In 1856, the Hunterian lectures were actually suspended in an attempt to make Owen direct more time to the work of cataloguing. There were disputes about where Owen should reside – under the terms of his employment, Owen was expected to reside on, or near, the premises. There is no doubt that Owen's rather difficult personality was part of the cause of these frictions, and he resented having to do some of the more routine curatorial work. Moreover, by the mid-1850s, Owen's scientific reputation was beginning to eclipse that of many of the administrators with whom he had to deal: 'there is not a more distinguished man of science in the country,' declaimed *The Times* on 25 January 1856. This acclaim probably rankled.

There were still more frustrations for Owen. Throughout much of the time that Owen was working at the Hunterian Museum, space was at a premium. The initial building from 1813 was inadequate by the 1830s; in 1833, a grant was obtained for the demolition of much of the existing accommodation so that the total amount of space for the museum might be increased. Expansions of the work of the college and of the collections was such that yet another exhibition area was completed in 1852, part of the great Victorian era's expansion of the public building inventory of London. During the periods of reconstruction, however, the ongoing disruption would have been very difficult for the curatorial staff.

Owen's ambition was for the Hunterian Museum to be the primary central national repository for the collections of comparative anatomy, osteology (the study of bones and skeletons) and palaeontology specimens, along with their study. More than once, he suggested that the Hunterian fossil collection should be combined with that of the British Museum, and he believed that the collections should be displayed in a set of buildings of appropriate grandeur. Owen obviously compared the importance of his institution with some of those on the continent. He hoped that the fossil collections of the British Museum would be transferred to new and grander buildings, and he actively lobbied parliamentarians and other influential persons in the hopes of realizing this dream.

Not unsurprisingly, some of the dignitaries of the college and museum resented when Owen went over their heads on occasion. However, the Treasury baulked at the cost and the two institutions remained separate. There was also the view that the then existing link between the natural history collections and the British Museum Library was of value.

Clearly these frustrations irritated Owen, and in the early 1850s he considered taking other appointments. One of these was as the professor of natural history at Edinburgh University, succeeding Edward Forbes in 1854. Owen knew Edinburgh, of course, and was urged to accept the post: he would have doubled his salary; he enjoyed lecturing and seems to have been good at it. However, he would have been required to reside in Edinburgh for most of the year, and he would have been separated from his beloved collections. After some negotiation, he withdrew his candidature.

G. H. Lewes wrote a somewhat hagiographical review of Owen's life and work in *Fraser's Magazine*, in 1856. In this review, one question was asked: 'We have a magnificent collection in the British Museum, and an unrivalled expositor in Professor Owen – why are the two separated?' Others of a Whig, Liberal or Progressive outlook offered their agreement. The man in charge of the British Museum and its library was one Antonio Panizzi, a strong-willed man who cared little for natural history. He was a wholehearted Arts scholar. Sculpture galleries and rare book collections were more important to him than fossils, minerals, plants or animals. Thus the representation of scientific thought in the British Museum's administration was widely seen to be inadequate.

On 26 May 1856 Richard Owen was offered the post of superintendent of the natural history department, at a proposed salary of £800 per annum. Although such a post was necessary, it was, to some extent, specially created for him. There were those in government who saw him as a brilliant and distinguished scientist, languishing on a niggardly remuneration in a post where he was not fully appreciated. However, the decision was the right one, for, at that time, the British Museum subtended over art and archaeology, as well as natural history; giving the latter its own autonomy and dignity was probably inevitable.

In some ways, Owen was supremely qualified for the job. Not only did he have a brilliant scientific record, he was also thoroughly familiar with the business of managing a museum, including the responsibilities of renovating and extending buildings and the tasks of curation. Moreover, he was experienced in dealing with restrictions regarding space. Parts of the zoology collection, among others, were described as 'jam-packed'. In 1858 John Jones, the keeper of printed books at the museum, commented that it was becoming 'a gigantic warehouse of unpacked goods'. A few years earlier, the palaeontologist Gideon Mantell had taken his children to see the exhibits; he found one of his own donations, a bone from a *Hylaeosaurus*, lying on the floor, smashed into pieces. He wrote in his diary of the 'scandalous manner' in which the material stored in the 'national collection is neglected'. New accommodation for the scientific collection was desperately needed. Arguments about whether the buildings on the existing Bloomsbury site should be expanded or a new site developed went on for years. 'I love Bloomsbury much,' wrote Owen at one juncture, 'but I love five acres more.' Since the early 1850s, the government had designated Kensington as a possible site for museum development.

Owen had a further skill: he seems to have been an experienced and quite accomplished lobbyist. Although not always successful, he was at ease in the presence of influential people – parliamentarians, academics and aristocrats – and when pleading his cause for funds. Within months of his accepting the appointment as superintendent of the natural history collections, these skills were put to work. He wanted the natural history section of the museum to be separated from that concerned with art and archaeology, and he wanted more room. He wanted a museum that would do justice to what he saw as the premier scientific organization in London – an institution that was fitting for a great imperial power. Following the publication of *On the Origin*, relations with Darwin had deteriorated badly, but Owen was not above using Darwin's publication and name as a part of his lobbying. He argued before a parliamentary committee that the whole intellectual world this year has been excited by a book on the origin of species; and what is the consequence? Visitors come to the British Museum, and they say, 'Let us see all these varieties of pigeons; where is the tumbler? Where is the pouter?' and I am obliged to say, I can show you none of them . . . As to showing you the varieties of those species, or any of those phenomena that would aid one in getting at the mystery of mysteries, the origin of species, our space does not permit.[6]

The public was curious to know about the theory of evolution, but the natural history collections of the British Museum were not able to respond adequately to the public's thirst for knowledge on such matters.

In January 1860 the trustees of the museum voted, with a single-vote majority, for the separation. Chairing the meeting was the prime minister, Lord Palmerston, and six of the nine votes in favour were cabinet ministers whom Lord Palmerston had brought into the meeting, even though previously they had seldom attended meetings of the trustees.

The board of trustees at around that time was what might be called a self-perpetuating oligarchy. Owen's biographer Nicolaas A. Rupke summarized the situation succinctly, regarding a slightly earlier time:

[The Board] was composed of forty-eight members. One trustee was directly appointed by the Crown. Twenty-three were *ex officio* trustees who were prominent members of the government, the Church and the judiciary . . . Nine trustees were representatives of families that had made major donations to the British Museum, such as, for example the Sloane, Cotton, Harley and Elgin families. A further fifteen members were elected trustees, chosen by the others. Nearly all family and elected members were aristocrats, among whom were several dukes, marquises and earls. Museum appointments came under the patronage of three principal trustees: the Archbishop of Canterbury, the Lord Chancellor and the Speaker of the House of Commons.[7]

It must be said that this was just the sort of society that Owen enjoyed; as we have seen, he had something of a penchant for the society of aristocrats.

Often few, if any, of the trustees were naturalists, and so the necessary separation of the natural history collections from those of art and archaeology was long delayed. Throughout much of the 1840s, '50s and '60s, many prominent scientists – Owen, Darwin, Huxley, Hooker, Sedgwick and Lyell among them – made representations to the government, stressing both the need for persons with some scientific knowledge to be appointed to the board of trustees and also the removal of the natural history collections to a separate site.

The following excerpt, part of a 'memorial' signed by two dozen eminent scientists, was delivered to the Chancellor of the Exchequer in 1866:

> We are of the opinion that it is of fundamental importance to the progress of the Natural Sciences in this country that the administration of the National Natural History Collections should be separated from that of the Library and Art Collections, and placed under one Officer, who should be immediately responsible to one of the Queen's Ministers.[8]

Comparisons were sometimes made with the Royal Observatory and Kew Gardens, which had their own separate existence as independent entities.

Owen's task as he struggled to establish a separate entity – that of a National Natural History Museum – was a difficult one. Both in his position of conservator at the Hunterian Museum and later, when in charge of the Natural History collections at the British Museum after 1856, he had to deal with a board of trustees, of which he was not a member but instead merely a paid employee. Indeed, a few individuals were members of both boards. It has been pointed out that Owen, although he played a part in the social ranks in which such people moved, was not of their ranks, in terms of the manner of his education, background or social position. He had, therefore, to accord appropriate respect to the aristocratic, clerical and medical hierarchies with which he came into contact, although he hoped that, in the long term, he would not always have to be subservient and would eventually be in charge of his own museum. This is probably part of the explanation as to why Owen was such a firm friend of the Reverend Professor William Buckland, who was educated at Winchester College and Corpus Christi, Oxford, and who was, in due course, Canon of Christ Church, Oxford, later becoming the Dean of Westminster. Buckland was trained in geology and worked on fossils, including dinosaurs; he also established that fossil bones in Kirkdale Cave, Yorkshire, proved that it had once been a hyena den. He was an FRS and was awarded the Copley Medal of the Royal Society. With sound Oxbridge and ecclesiastical credentials, Buckland not only understood the language that Owen was speaking but had an entrée to the right circles.

William Gladstone (also a Christ Church alumnus) was a strong supporter of the idea of an entirely new museum of natural history, and there was considerable correspondence between him and Owen. In October 1861 Gladstone accompanied Owen on a tour of the Bloomsbury site, to see for himself the nature of the problems of finding space. The two of them 'explored every vault and dark recess'. 'The Grand Old Man' was sympathetic, but time after time Parliament rejected the proposal for a new building on the grounds of cost. Over that decade, Owen rehearsed a number of arguments. On one occasion he made a not particularly veiled reference to Britain's imperial role:

> The annual additions of specimens continued to increase in number and value year by year. I embraced every opportunity to excite interest of intelligent settlers in our several colonies, to this end, among the results which I may cite the reception of the aye-aye, the gorilla, the dodo [from Mauritius], the Notornis [from New Zealand], the maximised and elephant-footed species of Dinornis [also from New Zealand], the representation of the various orders and genera of extinct Reptilia from the Cape of

William Ewart Gladstone, *c.* 1858: 'the people's William'.

Good Hope and the equally rich and numerous evidences of the extinct Marsupialia from Australia.[9]

Ultimately something of a strange alliance between Antonio Panizzi, of the British Museum, and Owen decided the matter. Panizzi ridiculed the plans that Owen had drawn up for the extension of the old Bloomsbury building and supported the move to Kensington; his motive was to get the natural history materials, as well as the scientists working with them, from under his feet.

Buckland was a supporter of Owen's plans for the Natural History Museum and had provided encouragement at several times during Owen's career. For example, Buckland sought a statement on his scientific work from Owen, as well as a note regarding his future plans. This, he submitted, accompanied by a glowing letter of support, to Sir Robert Peel (1788–1850), who was at that time the prime minister and, also, a Christ Church man. A Civil List pension of £200 per annum was forthcoming on 1 November 1842.

Let us now return to the construction of the National Natural History Museum – originally the British Museum (Natural History). In 1864, Francis Fowke, the architect of the Royal Albert Hall and portions of the Victoria and Albert Museum, won the competition to design the new museum. However, he died a year later and a much less well-known individual, the Liverpool architect Alfred Waterhouse, was invited to come up with plans for the new site in South Kensington. The resulting edifice is one of the United Kingdom's most striking examples of Victorian Romanesque architecture. Waterhouse used terracotta extensively for the exterior, which was resistant to the damaging effects of London's polluted climate.

He also incorporated a series of plant and animal images while, at the same time, keeping the design somewhat ecclesiastical; the main entrance closely resembles the entrance to a great medieval Gothic cathedral. Owen and Waterhouse co-operated to produce a worthy design for a 'Cathedral to Nature', a nod to the very Victorian doctrine of natural theology – the notion that nature's complexity and beauty provided evidence for the existence of a Creator God, as expounded by William Paley. The 'Book of Nature' complemented the 'Book of God' – the Bible. Owen introduced his address to the British Association in Leeds, in 1858, with the words: 'God has given to man a capacity to discover and comprehend the laws by which His universe is governed.' Owen's later remarks in this speech illustrate his thinking:

The simplest coral and the meanest insect may have something in history worth knowing, and in some way profitable. Every organism is a character in which Divine wisdom is written, and

ought to be expounded. Our present system of opening the
book of Nature to the masses, as in the galleries of the British
Museum, without any provision for expounding her language,
is akin to that which would keep the book of God sealed to the
multitude in a dead tongue.[10]

The establishment of a national museum of natural history is
almost portrayed as a task ordained by God – a divine duty. Work
on the new building began in 1873 and was completed in 1880. The
new museum opened in 1881, although moving all the collections
from the old Bloomsbury site was not fully completed until 1883.
Owen retired at the end of 1883, after 57 years of service to London's
museums.

Despite Richard Owen's enormous commitment to his museum
work, and his powerful research and publication record, he was a
staunch committee member. One of the most significant honours
accorded to Owen was his appointment to a committee planning
the Great Exhibition of 1851, chaired by Prince Albert himself. The
first meeting of the committee, which, apart from Owen, numbered
Lord Granville, Lord Stanley, Lyell, Henry Thomas De la Beche and
others among its members, was held at Buckingham Palace on
13 February 1850.[11]

Natural History Museum, London, late 19th century.

Owen was in his element; he liked nothing better than mingling with royalty, the aristocracy and 'the leading men of science'. He described the 'amusing variety of chat', following a lecture he gave to the royal children some years later: 'The Dean of Windsor . . . was present with all the Court, and Highnesses, both Serene and Royal . . . After their Majesties' departure, there is of course much chat with the lords and ladies in waiting.' Owen loved it. In March 1850, as the Great Exhibition work was beginning, he attended his first levee, where he was formally presented to the Prince Consort by the Earl of Carlisle. Later he was placed on a committee for the section of the exhibition dealing with 'Raw materials and produce of the animal kingdom' and was then on one of the juries of the exhibition. The work of preparing for the exhibition continued for many months; Owen was the 'Chairman of Jury IV', having the task of deciding which exhibit should receive awards. He was very proud when on 1 May 1851 he was invited with his family to attend the opening of the Great Exhibition, amidst much pomp and in the presence of Queen Victoria, Prince Albert and the Prince of Wales. After the closure of the exhibition, Owen wrote letters urging that the Crystal Palace be preserved. A few years later, he undertook similar committee work and service as a juror for the Paris Exhibition of 1855; this gave him the opportunity to mingle with the remnants of the French aristocracy.

At the same time as he was sitting on committees associated with the planning of the Great Exhibition, Owen was also on the Smithfield Commission on the Meat Supply of London. Many of those on this panel were all for 'patching up' the existing unsatisfactory situation, 'instead of doing away with it' and starting again on a separate site. As with so many things, Owen had strong opinions on the matter. It is recorded that:

> R[ichard] sat there boiling with indignation, till his turn came to give his opinion, and then he gave forth his protest against this new proposal in unmistakable language . . . It seems an obvious piece of stupidity to meet a reform by a proposal to perpetuate and increase the nuisance at an enormous outlay of money.[12]

He particularly disapproved of having slaughterhouses sited very close to the markets.

The Smithfield Commission was in fact the third in a series of strongly utilitarian government bodies on which Owen served in the latter part of the 1840s and early 1850s. The first was the Royal Commission inquiring into the State of Large Towns and Populous Districts, sometimes referred to as the Public Health of Towns Commission, which issued reports in 1844 and 1845. One of Richard Owen's particular tasks was to report on his native town of Lancaster; his 1845 report dealt with drainage, sewerage and water supply, as well as with mortality statistics. The chair of this body was the Duke of Buccleuch. The second government body on which Owen served was the Metropolitan Sanitary Commission, the full title of which was the Royal Commission on the Improvement of the Health of the Metropolis (1847–8).

Serving on these commissions brought Owen into contact with practical men of the ilk of Robert Stevenson, the engineer, and the head of the Geological Survey, De la Beche, as well as William Cubitt, the Lord Mayor of London. Membership of these august committees, besides giving Owen the chance to demonstrate his role in serving the community and using science for the benefit of the public, also allowed further opportunities for Owen to mingle with the great and the good of Victorian society. Sometimes, Owen was in a position to influence those who held real power and who might be able to use their good offices to support his museum ventures. Some of those with whom he worked in these settings were on the boards of trustees of the Hunterian Museum and the British Museum, and were, thus, of real importance to his career.

Another platform that Owen used, or hoped to use, for advancing his prestige was his membership of London clubs; as Rupke put it: 'By being able to meet and mix with the membership of the select clubs, one became part of the social networks that dominated Victorian socio-political and intellectual life.' He was elected to the highly prestigious Athenaeum Club in 1840, at the relatively young age of 36. He was proposed for membership by Viscount Cole, later the Earl of Enniskillen, who just happened to have been Buckland's pupil at Oxford. Richard Owen was admitted on 20 May 1845, at the same time as George Villiers, the 4th Earl of Clarendon, a diplomat and statesman.

Nothing succeeds like success, and in the years immediately following his election to the Athenaeum, Owen was invited to join two exclusive literary dining clubs. In 1844, he was elected to the dining club of the Literary Society, and, in 1845, to what has been described as 'the most prestigious dining club of all' – The Literary Club, Dr Johnson's Club, or just 'The Club'. It was founded in February 1764 by the artist Sir Joshua Reynolds, the essayist Dr Samuel Johnson and the Irishman Edmund Burke, a political philosopher. A list dated March 1879, when Richard Owen was 'the Father of the Club', shows the membership as limited to forty, including three dukes, one marquess, eleven lords and earls, and eight knights of the realm. The Church was represented by the Archbishop of Canterbury and the Dean of Westminster, science was represented by Sir Joseph Hooker, and literature by Alfred Tennyson. William Gladstone, the former prime minister (then in opposition), was also a member. Owen had found a place here, mingling with the intellectual and political elite of Victorian society.

This was not the only organization Owen attended that was frequented by the distinguished and the aristocratic. On 15 January 1866 Owen wrote that he 'went to dine at the Garrick Club. Many old friends there – Mr John Murray [publisher] M. Du Chaillu [explorer], Mr Pentland &c. Our bust of Shakespeare, which was bought by the Duke of Devonshire and presented to the Club, looked very well.'[13]

Owen's work at the Hunterian Collection and, later, at the British Museum, his community work on the commissions and other official enquiries, and his personal associations through his London dining clubs and similar institutions were closely linked to one another. There was considerable cross-membership. Those with whom Richard Owen mixed when serving on official enquiries and in his London clubs included members of the boards of trustees of the two museums; some also had close ties to Parliament and the sources of official funding. Owen clearly enjoyed his associations with his aristocratic friends, but he would have argued that when dining with bishops, earls and dukes – who were members of the Upper House of Parliament – he was seeking to further the interests of science.

However, one must not be too cynical: there were occasions where Owen campaigned on behalf of causes that could not possibly occasion any advantage to himself or to projects with which he was associated. He joined with Charles Dickens in opposing public executions and, indeed, on one occasion, wrote to the Home Secretary, Sir George Grey; he personally attended the Home Office to campaign on behalf of a young woman named Maria Clark who was under a sentence of death for child murder. Owen's view was that 'the poor creature was certainly not in her right senses from pain, and exposure to bad weather for twenty hours, and that she was therefore not to be considered a wilful criminal.' She was reprieved.

He also joined the campaign opposing the window tax, pointing out that in his medical opinion, light and proper ventilation were essential to the health of the population.

9

A Cottage in Richmond Park, by
Grace and Favour of Her Majesty

Richard Owen received an enormous range of honours in his lifetime; after his election to a Fellowship of the Royal Society at a comparatively early age, he gave the Bakerian Lecture in 1844 on belemnites and was awarded the Bakerian Medal. He was awarded the Royal Medal (1846) and the Copley Medal (1851) given by the same society. The Geological Society awarded him the Wollaston Medal as early as 1838; the Baly Medal from the Royal College of Physicians followed, in 1869. The Linnean Society also awarded him its eponymous medal in 1888.

Honorary degrees were heaped upon him in a cascade; first came Edinburgh (whereat he had studied for only a few months) in 1849, awarding him an LLD, followed by Oxford, with a DCL in 1852, and then Cambridge (LLD) in 1869. On 25 January 1856, *The Times* pronounced that there was 'not a more distinguished man of science in the country' than Richard Owen.

Owen's position in London, at the heart of the British Empire, meant that he was sent fossils and other specimens from various parts of the world; as a result of his work, many countries of the empire honoured him; the W. B. Clarke Medal of the Royal Society of New South Wales was given in 1878 (its first award). A silver medal came from the New Zealand Exhibition in 1865, with another from the Sydney Exhibition of 1879 and a bronze medal from Adelaide in 1887. A stream of honorary memberships and associateships came from learned societies on the continent – especially from France, recalling the link with Cuvier – but they were also received from Germany, Russia, Sweden, the Netherlands and Italy. The 'List of

Richard Owen's Honorary Distinctions' in the biography by his grandson includes nearly one hundred awards and honours.[1]

In 1843 the prime minister, Sir Robert Peel, awarded him a Civil List pension of £200 a year; Richard frequently complained that he was under-remunerated and so this provided a certain leavening of the situation, besides being a sign of his recognition in the highest circles.

However, there were hesitations in the general advance. When he was awarded a medal for the paper on belemnites, Owen failed to acknowledge that one specimen had initially been discovered by an amateur naturalist. Other accusations of plagiarism and inappropriate behaviour occurred, along with instances of bullying or the abuse of his position. For example, although, at an early stage in his career, Owen was supportive of the Royal Botanic Gardens at Kew and the attached herbarium, as he increasingly adopted an anti-Darwin stance he became ever more antagonistic towards that institution. Owen (supported by a notoriously difficult and arrogant MP, Acton Smee Ayrton) maintained that the Kew Herbarium should become subordinate to the British Museum and, therefore, to Owen, as the superintendent of the Natural History collections at that museum. Darwin's great friend and colleague Joseph Hooker, first the assistant director of Kew (1855–65) and then its director (1865–1905), was at one stage on the point of resigning the directorship. Owen's attitude and ungentlemanly behaviour eventually resulted in him being voted off the councils of the Royal Society, together with those of the Geological Society and the Zoological Society.

On 24 July 1845, just after Richard Owen's 41st birthday, Sir Robert Peel sent a message to Owen asking him whether he would accept a knighthood.[2] Mrs Owen wrote about the occasion in her diary: 'After talking [over] the matter with me, R[ichard] declined, as I desired. It would not add much to our comfort or respectability, and if the time should come when the collection had become part of a great national museum, then it might all be very well.'[3]

The Hunterian Collection never did become part of 'a great national museum', but eventually, Owen did become the superintendent of such an institution when he was appointed to the management of the Natural History collection of the British Museum, eventually overseeing the transfer of the collections to the new 'Cathedral of Science' in South Kensington in 1883. Owen was made a Knight Commander of the Order of the Bath in 1884; in recognition of this honour, the prime minister William Gladstone increased his Civil List pension by £100 per annum.

Always having enjoyed the company of the aristocracy, Owen was also quite an intimate of the royal family, ever since his time working with Prince Albert in the lead-up to the Great Exhibition in 1851. In April 1860 Owen 'gave by request of the Prince Consort some lectures to the Royal children at Buckingham Palace':

> Sir James [Clark] had a drawing room at Buckingham Palace fitted up . . . Sofas and armchairs are arranged in a semi-circle . . . The Prince enters with the children: one day I had the Prince of Wales, on other days all that remain at home; the young Duke of Edinburgh is among them, and I try to make as much of my discourse suitable to him as I can, and generally introduce two or three anecdotes for the younger children. They are all attentive and seem often to be deeply interested; and much of [what] I have had to say was evidently new to all . . . The three young Princesses are very sweet and unaffected in their manner.[4]

Owen gave the royal children successive lectures about mammals, birds, insects, fishes and other marine creatures. The talks were extremely well received and bore fruit shortly afterwards. Prince Alfred, Queen Victoria's second son and fourth child, joined the Royal Navy (apparently at his own request) at the age of twelve in 1856. Appointed midshipman on HMS *Euryalus*, he made a favourable impression when the ship visited Cape Colony in 1860. As well as taking part in 'the slaughter of a large number of game animals', he came across or was given the skull of a fossil *Dicynodont* reptile and other fossil remains from the South African Karoo formation. Richard Owen was called upon to describe these; he discussed them in a paper published in the

Prince Albert, Queen Victoria's consort and a supporter of science, 1859.

Philosophical Transactions of the Royal Society in 1862. Owen sent a copy to the queen and received an appreciative reply from one of her staff, who remembered that the late Prince Albert had had 'a very high respect and regard' for Owen. This association continued and Owen gave another series of talks, this time at Windsor Castle, in March and April 1864.

Somewhat earlier, just before Christmas in 1851, Owen had received a letter informing him that 'a house upon Kew Green having become vacant . . . Her Majesty is happy in being able to offer this house as a residence for you'. There were various legal delays; when Richard Owen inspected the premises, he thought it was rather too palatial. After hearing that a smaller residence, sometimes referred to as 'a cottage', in Richmond Park was available, he managed to persuade Prince Albert that this might be more suitable. The Owens moved into Sheen Lodge, Richmond Park, on Saturday, 15 May 1852, his family making their 'first appearance at Mortlake Church the following day'.

Owen delighted in the country lifestyle that Richmond Park provided. Being awakened at three o'clock that first Sunday morning, he became aware of

> a concert of a very unusual kind to my ears, and, tempted by the unwonted strains I stole down into the garden. Day was grayly dawning in the northeast, and some light clouds floating across a pearly sky. The nightingales were sending forth interrupted capricious carols from every bush; with a higher treble for some unknown warblers, and a lower one for thrushes and blackbirds. The distant curlew kept up a running tenor accompaniment, and the more distant rookery gave out a steady bass; with the occasional addition of the wood-pigeon's plaintive coo-oo. Then came the echo of the cheery crow of a distant cock, the lowing of the steer, and the drowsy hum of the humble-bee. The air was fragrant with newly opening azaleas and whitethorn, and I was tempted to the brink of the little lake by the strange gambols and gyrations of the great black-backed carp.[5]

The birds in the garden at Sheen Lodge and the deer in Richmond Park were sources of great pleasure in Owen's later years. Sometimes, the well-known ornithologist John Gould (who had examined and reported on the bird specimens that Charles Darwin brought back from the *Beagle* voyage), would join him for a few hours of bird-watching. Owen kept a garden book in which he noted the details of some of the birds that he saw: the blue and great tits, the robins and sparrows, the rooks and the nightjars. Interestingly, there are accounts that occasionally touch briefly on the behaviour and ecology of organisms, a topic that is generally rather rare in Owen's writings. However, these short accounts are somewhat anthropomorphic, with the incidents being described in human terms. The 'throstle' or song thrush was the 'little robber' who stole Owen's cherries; the blue tit, 'mustering courage', darted towards a lump of suet; the 'pugnacious robin . . . takes his stand on the window-sill'.[6] Occasionally, Owen went fishing in the small lake.

If this sounds idyllic, it was. Some have hinted that his occupancy of the grace-and-favour residence of Sheen Lodge, together with his long association with the royal family, were the factors that made him hesitate to give support to Darwin's

FIG. 1.—SIR RICHARD OWEN'S COTTAGE. (SEE P. 8.)

Sir Richard Owen's cottage, Sheen Lodge, in Richmond Park, from *Gardeners' Chronicle*, 5 July 1890.

evolutionary ideas. There was clearly a deep personal antagonism between Owen and Darwin – and even more so with Huxley. Intellectually speaking, particularly later on, the two men were perhaps not so very far apart, but despite her late husband's enthusiasm for science, it is said that Queen Victoria had no love of Darwinism.

Owen had an extensive library containing modern novels as well as scientific works. The books were kept in what was described by his grandson as 'an old-fashioned room', with windows that overlooked Richmond Park in one direction and the garden in the other. Those walls of this room that were not filled with bookshelves bore 'medallions and miniatures' of the distinguished scientists and medical men that Owen himself had known, alongside those from the more remote past; these included Sir Isaac Newton, Baron Cuvier, John Hunter, Sir Joseph Banks and William Clift. They were accompanied – rather curiously, in view of his great affection for the royal family – by an image of Oliver Cromwell. Some of his scientific friends would visit him there; so too did a number of literary figures. Sometimes, Owen would play a game of chess with his visitors; he seems to have been a good player.

He would go for a daily walk around his garden, in later years being supported by a curiously carved stick. Part of the garden was given over to a small area of woodland, and the garden was decorated with a number of curiosities. There was a garden seat made from some of the vertebrae of a whale, and a crocodile skull grinned from a rockery. A plaster cast of an ancient Egyptian sculpture (Owen had visited Egypt several times) rested on a pedestal on the 'west walk'.

For much of the time that he lived in Richmond Park, Richard Owen would have commuted to central London, it being 9 kilometres (5½ mi.) to South Kensington and about 18 kilometres (11 mi.) to Bloomsbury, presumably travelling for the most part by carriage. However, Owen may not have gone to his workplace every day; he was oftentimes travelling outside London for meetings and he sometimes went abroad (to Switzerland and Germany; he also paid several visits to the Mediterranean and Egypt).

Owen described Caroline as his great helpmate; she assisted him with his work, her artistic talents being particularly useful. They celebrated their silver wedding day with great happiness at the Lodge, and received many gifts of silverware, this occasion falling on the same day as Richard's 56th birthday, 20 July 1860.

Caroline does not seem to have been included in many of his travels; on his return from an excursion to Egypt, Malta and Italy, on 15 March 1873, he found his wife seriously ill, and she died on 7 May 1873. She was buried in the quiet churchyard of St Andrew's in the nearby village of Ham; Richard himself was eventually interred in the same churchyard. Alas, it was just a few days after Caroline's death that Owen received a letter from the prime minister, William Gladstone, offering him 'a choice of distinctions'; he selected that of the 'Companion of the Most Honourable Order of the Bath'.

Work on the new Natural History Museum continued, with Owen's close supervision. Although Owen was previously a prolific correspondent, his friends and colleagues found that after his wife's death, his letters became far less frequent. He was clearly lonely; around October 1873, his sister, Maria, came to keep house for him. They seem to have always been close; Richard had frequently written to his sister, describing his activities and the distinguished people he had met.

In 1883, Owen wrote in his diary: 'With this year [I] end my official relations with the national collections of natural history, the several departments – Zoology, Geology, Fossils, Minerals, Plants – being arranged and displayed in their respective galleries. I felt that I could "depart in peace", for mine eyes had seen their salvation.'[7] His knighthood was finally gazetted on 5 January 1884.

Around that time, a change of focus and a slight narrowing of Owen's horizons is perhaps symbolized by the fact that one of his publications, listed for 1883, was entitled 'Notes on Birds in the Garden, Sheen Lodge, Richmond Park', published in a periodical called *The Garden*. Nevertheless, his output of research publications continued: ten publications are listed for 1884, although one was a reprint of earlier papers on fossil reptiles. However, his output soon after declined: for 1885, he had three publications; for 1886 and 1887,

Richard Owen with his granddaughter Emily, *c.* 1890, engraving based on a
photograph.

he published four each year; for 1888 and 1889, it was three each year. None is recorded after that date. His regular attendance at the meeting of the British Association for the Advancement of Science seems to have become more irregular after 1882.

Owen's son William died in 1886, and another sister soon after that. His eldest grandson lived with him at Sheen Lodge until 1889, when his daughter-in-law and the remainder of her children joined him. Owen became much weaker and increasingly deaf. A letter to his grandson Richard (who was studying at Cambridge), dated October 1887, illustrates the tempo of these later years:

> I enjoyed a charming dinner at White Lodge [nearby in Richmond Park, and the home of the Duke and Duchess of Teck] since you left for Cambridge, but time passes very quietly and peacefully with me at home; a brief sunshine occasionally tempts me round the garden. I can hardly think of a more thank-worthy condition at the close of a busy life than that which I am now enjoying.[8]

Some of his scientific and literary friends continued to visit him; so too did the Duke and Duchess of Teck, as well as the Prince of Wales; his earlier links with the royal family were fondly remembered.

Owen's weakness became severe in November and December 1892, and 'A little before three o'clock on Sunday morning, 19 December 1892, he passed peacefully away.' Shortly before his death, he had been assured by Queen Victoria that his family would continue to live at Sheen Lodge after his demise.

He was survived by his daughter-in-law, Emily Owen (to whom he left much of his estate of about £33,000), and by his three grandchildren.

Not long after his death, a committee was set up to look into the possibility of honouring Owen with a suitable memorial. Some 330 donations were received from the great and the good of British science. The committee was chaired by the Prince of Wales, and over £1,100 was raised.[9] Eventually a bronze statue was commissioned and erected in the Natural History Museum.

10

Owen's Character and Personality

Any attempt to diagnose the mental state of those that are long dead is fraught with difficulties; the individual is not available for scrutiny, and the information collected during the subject's lifetime may be very incomplete and may have been accumulated (and perhaps, to some extent, assessed) at a time when the understanding of psychology and indeed psychiatry was very different from today. The subject under study is unavailable for interview and although one may sometimes have quite detailed contemporary written accounts of their behaviour, these may be derived from biased or partisan sources. There are those who say that such attempts must be doomed to failure; nevertheless, they have quite often been made. Charles Darwin's medical and psychological history has been much discussed, and suggestions have been made as to the manner in which his personality may have contributed to his delay in publishing his evolutionary ideas. One example of a biography of Darwin written by an eminent psychiatrist is *Charles Darwin: A New Biography* (1990).[1] In this account, John Bowlby attempted to show that for several decades the great Victorian naturalist suffered from acute psychosomatic illness, triggered by incidents in Darwin's childhood, bereavements and the stresses brought on by his scientific work. This approach has received a measure of support in recent years; recently, P. van Helvert and J. van Wyhe have listed a whole series of attempted explanations for Darwin's symptoms, both psychological and organic, including depressive psychosis, panic disorder, obsessive-compulsive disorder and Asperger's syndrome.[2] More recently, Ioan James, FRS, a distinguished Oxford mathematician, has suggested that some of the world's most brilliant scientists, including Isaac Newton, Henry Cavendish and Albert Einstein, might have been 'on the autism spectrum'.[3]

Richard Owen was in many respects a larger-than-life individual; thus a tentative attempt at an evaluation of his mental attributes and character seems to be worthwhile.

He was clearly very highly intelligent; this fact seems to have been recognized by John Barclay, his teacher at Edinburgh, and by John Abernethy when he arrived in London. He was one of the most brilliant and productive men in British (and European) science in the nineteenth century, gaining a string of outstanding awards. He was an FRS by the time he was thirty and gained a whole series of medals for his contributions to the natural sciences, as well as honorary degrees from several universities. He was awarded honours by scientific societies all over the world. Even his enemies, for example, Darwin and Huxley, used words such as 'clever' to describe him.

A phenomenally hard worker, his contributions to anatomical science, medicine and palaeontology included many hundreds of papers. These days, he would perhaps be described as a workaholic; his grandson referred to him as having 'incessant work on his hands'. There is also abundant evidence that Owen was a difficult individual.

The tentative suggestion is that Owen showed some of the characteristics of narcissistic personality disorder (NPD) or at least some of the related narcissistic personality traits. One authoritative source on mental assessment and the identification of psychological traits can be found in the *Psychodynamic Diagnostic Manual*:

> The characteristic . . . of narcissistic individuals is . . . [one that] requires recurrent infusions of external confirmation of their importance and value . . . When the narcissistic individual succeeds in extracting such confirmation in the form of status, admiration, wealth and success, he or she feels an internal elation, often behaves in a grandiose manner, and treats others (especially those perceived to be of lower status) with contempt

. . . [Such] individuals tend to defend their wounded self-esteem through a combination of idealising and devaluing others. When they idealise someone, they feel more special or important by virtue of their association with him or her. When they devalue someone, they feel superior.[4]

The psychological literature more broadly suggests that a person with a narcissistic personality disorder may possess several of the following criteria:

– Grandiosity, with the expectation of superior treatment from other people;
– Continually demeaning, bullying and belittling others;
– Exploiting others for personal gain or advantage;
– A lack of empathy, particularly in relation to the negative impact that their behaviour has on the feelings, wishes and needs of others;
– Fixation on fantasies of power, success, intelligence and attractiveness;
– Self-perception of being unique, superior and associated with high-status people and institutions;
– A need for constant admiration from others;
– A sense of entitlement to special treatment and to obedience from others;
– Intense envy of others, and the belief that others are equally envious of them.[5]

Although not all these characteristics are apparent in what we know of Richard Owen, several of them are recognizable, at least to some degree.

With those with whom he disagreed, or who disagreed with him – the likes of Darwin, Huxley and Hooker – Owen made his contempt very clear, belittling their work in print or in the lecture-hall. Conversely, he loved to associate with the great and the good. Association with dignitaries of the Church (deans and bishops) and members of the aristocracy (baronets, viscounts, earls, marquesses and dukes) was an addictive elixir. Owen greatly loved associating with 'high-status individuals and institutions'. He rejoiced in his election to prestigious London clubs such as the Athenaeum, and the Literary Club, or the Club. At times brilliantly intellectual, the membership, traditionally limited to forty members, included numerous members of the aristocracy.

For example, in a letter to one of his sisters in February 1866, following his return from dinner at the Club, Owen reported:

> I sat next [to] the Premier and opposite the Lord Chancellor.
> The Duke of Argyll was in the chair, supported by the Duc d'Aumale and the Dean of Westminster: then Lord Stanhope, Lord Kingsdown, Sir H. Holland, Froude, Dean Milman, Mr Stirling, Sir Edward Head, Spencer, Walpole, and the Editor of the Edinburgh Review (Reeve) . . . Lord Russell and I talked about our gardens [and] primroses.[6]

In 1879, the year in which Richard Owen became the senior member (according to his date of election), the membership included three dukes (Cleveland, Argyll, D'Aumale), a marquess (Salisbury), four earls and half a dozen knights of the realm. The Church was represented by the Dean of Westminster and the Archbishop of Canterbury. William Ewart Gladstone (four times prime minister) had been elected to the Club in March 1857.

Owen was certainly very conscious of his own importance. He greatly enjoyed lecturing and was good at it; the geologist Roderick Murchison, on one occasion, remarked of one of his orations: 'I never heard so thoroughly eloquent a lecture.'[7] Owen usually lectured in an academic gown; he loved an audience. Time and again, in his letters, he comments on how much his lectures were appreciated by his audiences. In a letter to his wife, addressed from Bradford, Yorkshire, and dated 16 November 1867, Owen writes: 'On Tuesday and Thursday, we drove to the Lecture Hall at 8.30 each day and got back after 10; I slept well, after holding forth to large and apparently gratified audiences.'[8] A day or two later, at another function in the same town, when Owen entered to take his place on the platform, he received a rapturous round of applause. Possibly, his prodigious publication record can also be seen as a manifestation of his constant need for self-validation; put at the most basic level, he liked to see his name in print.

Perhaps part of Owen's story can be traced back to his childhood and youth. NPD is sometimes said to be associated with a lonely, disrupted or traumatic childhood. Richard Owen came from an undistinguished, although not particularly deprived, background. His father died when he was a small child and there is some slight evidence that he was absent before that. However, Owen had an elder brother and several sisters; the brother seems to have left for the West Indies quite early and died young while he was out there. At an early age, Owen was apprenticed to a surgeon-apothecary; assisting with post-mortems in the grim and draughty Lancaster Castle Gaol must have been quite traumatic for a young teenager. There was also the 'headless man' incident. His apprenticeship was transferred several times – this would certainly have been disruptive for him. He attended Edinburgh University for only a few months and then headed for London, where he initially seems to have felt somewhat lonely. There, he qualified as a surgeon, perhaps as much on the basis of his acquaintanceships as through any formal academic process.

Thus Owen started his career with few advantages: a few years at a local grammar school, rather than the Harrow, Winchester or Westminster schools of some of his scientific contemporaries. Edinburgh was worthy enough (after all, the male Darwins attended for several generations), but Christ Church, Oriel or Balliol in Oxford, or Trinity or Christ's College in Cambridge perhaps gave their alumni something a little different. And as we have seen, Darwin also described Owen as being 'jealous' of his success when *On the Origin* was published.

Many contemporaries described Owen as arrogant; he had difficulties in getting along with many (but not all) of his scientific colleagues. Some of his conduct verged on the dishonest, such as when he claimed professorial rank at the School of Mines while he was actually only a part-time visiting lecturer. Or when, on a number of occasions, he was accused of conduct unbecoming, ranging from failing to give credit to those who assisted him with his research to something close to out-and-out plagiarism. In 1846 he was awarded the Royal Society's Royal Medal for a paper he had written on belemnites – a type of fossil cephalopod. He had not acknowledged the finding of the belemnite by Joseph Chaning Pearce, a Wiltshire medical man and amateur geologist, some years earlier. The ensuing scandal caused him to be voted off the councils of several important scientific bodies.

He occasionally went to extraordinary lengths to belittle those whom he saw as his rivals; he was extremely conscious of his own position. Sometimes it seems as though he had a one-track mind regarding his own concerns and was very determined in the pursuit of his objective, no matter what consequences may have ensued (a characteristic that is sometimes considered a feature of autism). He did not react well to criticism or opposition; the way in which he pursued Gideon Mantell in a most vicious manner as far as, and even beyond, death is inexcusable and attracted much unfavourable comment.

Another of his *bêtes noires* was Hugh Falconer, a distinguished geologist and botanist who had produced important work regarding fossils from India. Owen disagreed with him during his lifetime, but, as in the case of Mantell, he continued the antagonism even after Falconer's death in 1865. In 1871 Richard Owen published a paper in the *Philosophical Transactions of the Royal Society* on Australian fossils, in particular, the 'marsupial lion' or thylacine. The paper was refereed by Peter M. Duncan, FRS, a fellow of the Geological Society and professor of geology at King's College, London. Duncan advised against publishing at least part of the paper, the portion that

refers to misunderstandings and old grievances resulting from publications which appeared . . . some years since, and which should have been buried with the dead and long since forgiven. There are many passages in this part which I am sure Prof Owen would regret to read in a few years' time, although it is evident that he now feels as strongly as ever the somewhat pointed

criticisms of his fellow labourer in comparative anatomy,
Dr Falconer. I regret to have to state that Prof Owen passes the
usual boundaries of discussion in dealing with Prof Flower's
opinions and writing, and that he even goes out of his way to
attack Prof Huxley.[9]

It is perhaps of note that William Flower succeeded Owen, both as
conservator at the Hunterian Museum and as superintendent of the
Natural History Museum.

In the latter part of his life, Owen was the superintendent of a
'Great National Museum' in London, the centre of the empire, and
he did not like his authority to be challenged. Those naturalists
who wrote from India, Australia or New Zealand – outposts of
the empire – were sometimes put firmly in their place by Owen.
Colonial naturalists were seen as mere collectors of specimens
and of information. The work of describing, interpreting and
concept-building was more appropriately performed by the likes
of Owen at the centre. Sir Thomas Mitchell (1792–1855), the
Scottish-born surveyor general for the colony of New South Wales,
sent fossil material to Owen, and there followed a series of articles
on extinct Australian mammals, some of them being of vast size.
These included *Diprotodon*, a large wombat, some specimens of
which have been found to be up to 1.8 metres (5 ft 11 in.) in height
and nearly 4 metres (13 ft) in length. The spectacular had always
appealed to Owen.

It should be noted that as time wore on, these colonial naturalists
became increasingly unhappy with this division of labour that
contributed to Owen's success. Institutions such as museums
and scientific societies developed in Australia, New Zealand and
elsewhere in the empire, and the separation between collecting and
description and evaluation became less marked.

We need only return to Owen's review of *On the Origin of
Species* in the *Edinburgh Review* for examples that seem to display
several of the characteristics mentioned in the preceding pages;
Owen's tone is frequently sarcastic. Darwin described the possible
interrelationships among red clover, bees (especially bumblebees),

mice (which destroy the combs and nests of bees) and cats. Darwin speculated that an increase in the number of cats might bring pressure to bear on the mouse population, allowing bumblebees to thrive, thereby benefiting the pollination of the clover.

Here is Owen's sarcastic retort regarding these theoretical speculations:

> This is very characteristic of the ingenious turn of thought of our author; *the more sober, or perhaps duller, naturalist would, no doubt, appreciate more highly a dry statement of investigation* of the actual extinction of red clover, and tracing that extinction inductively, by the ascertained absence of humble-bees and mice, back to the want of cats in the neighbourhood.[10] (Emphasis added)

To be fair, Darwin did not have observational detail to back this up, although the integrated, ecological approach was ahead of its time.

Complaining that Darwin did not have sufficient observational detail to back up his theory of natural selection (which was, of course, absurd), Owen expostulated:

> Failing the adequacy of such observations . . . we were left to confide in the superior grasp of mind, strength of intellect, clearness and precision of thought and expression, which raise one man so far above his contemporaries as to be able to discern in the common stock of facts, of coincidences, correlations and analogies in Natural History, deeper and truer conclusions than his fellow-labourers had been able to reach.[11]

Although the reviewer purported to be anonymous, it was clear who had written it. There are frequent comparisons of the work of *Professor* Owen to that of *Mr* Darwin. Owen is also referred to favourably and in a more definite-sounding, authoritative manner. The review abounds with phrases such as: 'Professor Owen and others . . . have more especially studied'; 'Professor Owen does not hesitate to state'; 'Professor Owen has pointed out'; 'Owen has shown that'; 'Professor Owen's last publication'. On the other hand, mentions of Darwin often included weasel words: 'Thus several, perhaps the majority, of younger naturalists have been *seduced* into the acceptance of the . . . transmutative hypothesis now *presented* to them by Mr Darwin'; 'It is *assumed* by Mr Darwin'.

After referring to Darwin's reference to humans' artificial selection of domestic plants and animals, which occupies many detailed pages of *On the Origin*, Owen dismissively remarks: 'instead of satisfying our craving with the mature fruit of inductive research, Mr Darwin offers us the intellectual husks above quoted, endorsed by his firm belief in their nutritive sufficiency.'[12]

Charles Darwin was not the only one to suffer from Owen's vitriol in this review. Thomas Huxley, in 1860, had recently given a lecture defending evolutionary ideas at the Royal Institution. Owen was scathing regarding the way in which

> members of the Royal Institution of Great Britain are taught by their evening lecturer that such a limited or inadequate view and treatment of the great problem, that exemplifies the application of science to which England owes its greatness, we take leave to remind the managers [of the Royal Institution], that it more truly parallels the abuse of science to which a neighbouring nation owed its temporary degradation. We gazed with amazement at the audacity of the dispenser of the hour's intellectual amusement, who, availing himself of the technical ignorance of his auditors sought to blind them as to the frail foundations of 'natural selection'.[13]

Not only is the management of the Royal Institution denigrated but the audience of its evening series of lectures, along, of course, with Huxley.

Of course, what a person writes may not give a completely fair impression of what they might say face-to-face or how they may behave, but the whole of this review is intended to put down Darwin and anyone who accepts his ideas or gives them a platform and aims at emphasizing the superiority of the author's own approach and his status.

Owen seems to have refused few opportunities to mingle with the great and the good. Sir Richard Owen's biographer and grandson, also called Richard Owen, made extensive use of contemporary letters and diaries and frequently referred to the distinguished people with whom Sir Richard was associating, at meetings, on government commissions or socially. There is every indication that Owen got on well with such people. He seems to have been exceedingly courteous in their company. To those who posed no threat to him and who acknowledged his expertise, he was extremely gracious. He liked literature and knew both Alfred, Lord Tennyson and Charles Dickens and got on well with at least some of the Oxbridge academic elite. Such people often seemed to warm to him. This is perhaps not an entire surprise; the *Psychodynamic Diagnostic Manual* suggests:

> Psychopathic individuals may be charming and even charismatic, and may read other's emotional states with great accuracy . . . [but] they typically lose interest in people they see as no longer useful to them . . . Their indifference to the feelings and needs of others, including their characteristic lack of remorse after damaging other people, probably reflects a grave disorder in early attachment.[14]

Perhaps 'psychopathic' is the wrong word to use; psychological conditions exist on a continuum from very mild to extremely severe, and Owen was certainly able to function in society. Nevertheless, he was often extremely self-centred. Interestingly, it does seem that with both Darwin and Huxley, relations were originally good, but when they were clearly seen to be following their own paths, the link soured.

Owen appreciated art, frequently visiting art galleries, and was quite musical, playing the cello well – indeed, he took some lessons when he was in Paris as a young man, and he often attended concerts. Moreover, he seems to have been a devoted and affectionate family man; by all accounts he loved his wife Caroline, his sisters and his son and grandson. He remained attached to his mother; when he was away from home, he wrote frequent and detailed letters to her and to other family members, describing what he was doing and – almost always – the people he met, especially if they were well-known, titled or distinguished in some way. His grandson, in the preface to his biography, confirms:

> His general character stands out clearly . . . and although from our relative ages it is impossible that I could have a personal knowledge of his private life until his later years, I can but repeat the unfailing testimony of his friends in regard to his charm of manner, his genial courtesy, and his kindness of heart. All this and a great deal more I have seen for myself.[15]

Of course, the testimony of a family member must be treated with caution. Yet there were many young scientists whom Owen supported, or for whom he wrote favourable references at early stages in their careers. He often helped younger naturalists along, by means of a favourable review of a paper they had written. He 'engineered the election' to the Athenaeum Club of John Gould, Darwin's bird man, 'the son of a gardener and a man without any advantages of education'. Owen's St Bartholomew's pupil William White Cooper (1816–1886), who later became a renowned ophthalmic surgeon, was quite gushing:

> Words are quite inadequate to describe the feelings of regard, of affection . . . I may say I entertain for you . . . You have filled that void in my heart which the death of my Father occasioned. You have been to me a Parent, and so long as I live . . . my heart will turn to you with feelings such as no language can express.[16]

It is as though there were two sides to his personality; he was the affable courteous intellectual in the company of those he deemed his equals (or his social superiors), those whom he saw as being useful to him, and members of his family and close friends. To these and to the young medic or naturalist who acknowledged him as the expert, and who paid appropriate deference to him, he was charming. But there was another side to Owen – the argumentative, petty, jealous, sometimes almost vicious and cunning individual who emerged when confronted by those he disliked, or whose opinions he did not share, or perhaps, very occasionally, whose opinions he did not dare to say that he shared.

There are two further points that suggest that the compartmentalizing and separation between the two sides of his personality was not quite complete and that his family life was not quite as idyllic as he sometimes portrayed. Richard Owen travelled widely, lecturing, seeking specimens for the museum and visiting colleagues and friends throughout Britain and a good deal of Europe. He spent some weeks in Switzerland, in August 1860, and described in great detail an ascent of the 'Cime de Jazi', a summit in the Monte Rosa range, giving vivid descriptions of the rough footpath, the guides, the ropes, the glaciers, snowfields and peaks and also a soaring eagle. He visited North Africa several times – on one trip to Egypt, he accompanied the Prince and Princess of Wales and the Duke of Sutherland. Yet his wife seldom seems to have travelled with him; his only son, William, committed suicide by jumping into the River Thames, although few details of the incident are available. (The family possibly hushed the matter up; all that appears in his grandson's biography are the words 'After the death of his only son in 1886'.) It has been hinted that this might have been a manifestation of a domineering father.

Owen had a unique personality: highly intelligent, driven by his work and ambitious in the extreme. The zeal with which he savagely attacked his enemies was obsessive, and there is evidence of obsessive behaviour in other spheres. In 1826 a production of the opera *Oberon; or, The Elf-King's Oath* (by Carl Maria von Weber) was put on at Covent Garden, and it is said that Owen attended it 31 times. There are indications of two distinct sides to his persona: the gracious, affectionate and sensitive aesthete and the arrogant, self-centred egoist, occasionally consumed by what almost amounts to malice. While Owen, definitely, displayed at least some of the characteristics of NPD, the complete separation of the two distinct personalities is perhaps less clear-cut.

A number of other symptoms are listed in the literature as the accompaniments of psychological disorders; these include sleep problems, alcohol and other substance abuse, amnesia, excessive anxiety and trance-like states. However, there is little evidence of any of these symptoms; Owen seems to have enjoyed good health throughout much of his life, although just after Christmas 1863 he wrote to a friend: 'For a wonder (and I can't be sufficiently thankful for having been free for so many years), I am tied to my house by sciatica in the left limb, which keeps me awake at night.'[17]

A little earlier, after a very strenuous trip to the Highlands of Scotland, he experienced a 'loss of muscular powers', which incapacitated him for a short time. Occasionally, he had trouble with his eyes, apparently due to working and reading in poor light. His grandson implies that he had almost 'altogether escaped illness', although in old age he became deaf, somewhat immobile and slightly absent-minded. As mentioned earlier, it is sometimes asserted that NPD can be traced back to trauma or abuse of some kind in youth. But of definite abuse, there is no evidence whatever. Could his exposure as a teenager to death, disease and the dissection of cadavers have had an effect? Again, there is little evidence; he seems to have positively thrived on such things.

Perhaps one had better just comment that Richard Owen had a fascinating, somewhat difficult and strange personality. He was certainly a unique individual.

Chronology

1804   Born in Lancaster, northern England

1809   Death of father

1810   Attends Lancaster Grammar School

1820   Leaves school; he is apprenticed to surgeon apothecaries in Lancaster and obtains his training in dissection

1824   Enters Edinburgh University Medical School

1825   Leaves Edinburgh and arrives at St Bartholomew's Hospital, London

1826   Achieves membership of the Royal College of Surgeons

1827   Appointed assistant curator at the Hunterian Museum, Royal College of Surgeons

1828   Appointed lecturer in comparative anatomy at St Bartholomew's Hospital and commences his lecturing career

1831   Visits Georges Cuvier in Paris

1832   Publishes *Pearly Nautilus*

1834   Elected as Fellow of the Royal Society

1835   Appointed as Professor of Comparative Anatomy at St Bartholomew's Hospital; marries Caroline Clift, the daughter of his superior at the Hunterian Museum, after a long engagement

1839   Publishes part 1 of the BAAS *Report on British Fossil Reptiles*; formation of the Microscopical Society of London, renamed the Royal Microscopical Society in 1866

1836   Appointed as the Hunterian Professor; son, William, is born. Owen commences co-operation with Charles Darwin over fossil South American mammals

1840   Publishes jointly with Darwin his work on fossil South American mammals

1842   Publishes part 2 of the revised BAAS *Report on British Fossil Reptiles*, in which he introduces the group of Dinosauria. Owen is given a Civil List pension of £200 a year, and is appointed as the Conservator at the Hunterian Museum

1843–6   Serves on the Commission of Inquiry into the Health of Towns

1844   Elected as a member of 'the Club', and declines a knighthood

1847   Publishes the BAAS *Report on the Archetype and Homologies of the Vertebrate Skeleton*

1847–8   Serves on the Metropolitan Sanitary Commission

1849   Serves on the panel for the Commission on Smithfield Market and the Meat Supply of London

1851   Appointed as chairman of one of the juries (raw materials and foods) for the Great Exhibition

1852   Moves with his family to a grace-and-favour residence, Sheen Lodge, in Richmond Park

1853   Presides over a dinner for men of science in the *Iguanodon* statue at Crystal Palace Gardens, Sydenham; appointed as the superintendent of the natural history collections of the British Museum

1857   Commences lectures at the Royal School of Mines; rivalry with Thomas Huxley begins

1858   Elected president of the Royal Society

1859   Charles Darwin publishes *On the Origin of Species*

1860   Lectures on natural history for the royal children at Buckingham Palace; publishes a vicious review of *On the Origin* anonymously. Relations between Darwin and Owen deteriorate

1863   Describes the *Archaeopteryx*

1864   Gives lectures to the royal family at Windsor Castle

1873   Death of wife, Caroline

1873–81   Erection of the new Natural History Museum in Kensington

1880–83   Supervises the removal of the natural history collections to the new museum

1883   Retires from the position of superintendent of the British Museum (Natural History)

1884   Accepts a knighthood

1886   Son, William Owen, commits suicide

1892   Dies at Sheen Lodge

1897   Bronze statue of Owen unveiled at the British Museum (Natural History)

References

Introduction

1 Britain's industrial expansion mirrored imperial development. The expansion of the railways and steamship lines enabled scientific colleagues to keep in touch with one another with much greater facility than theretofore. The introduction of the Penny Post in January 1840 further assisted their endeavours, offering efficient and cheap communication.

2 R. Owen, *The Zoology of the Voyage of HMS Beagle: Part I, Fossil Mammalia*, ed. C. Darwin (London, 1840).

3 R. Owen, *Memoir on the Pearly Nautilus* ('*Nautilus Pompilius', Linn.*) (London, 1832).

4 C. Darwin, *The Autobiography of Charles Darwin*, ed. Nora Barlow (London, 1958), pp. 104–5. Versions of this work are also published online, for instance, at www.darwin-online.org.uk.

5 Letter from C. Darwin to H. Falconer, 12 July 1860, in *The Correspondence of Charles Darwin*, vol. VIII: *1860*, ed. F. Burkhardt et al. (Cambridge, 1993), p. 285. Hereafter, *Correspondence*.

6 Lead diacetate (Pb(CH3CO2) 2) is a slightly sweet-tasting toxin.

7 R. S. Owen, *The Life of Richard Owen by His Grandson* (London, 1894), vol. II, pp. 166–7.

8 Quoted in N. A. Rupke, *Richard Owen, Victorian Naturalist* (New Haven, CT, and London, 1994), p. 7.

1 Northern Origins: Childhood and Early Life

1 Owen's reputation for impudence as a child was perhaps a precursor to his being described as 'arrogant' and 'self-opinionated' in later life.
2 R. S. Owen, *The Life of Richard Owen by His Grandson* (London, 1894), vol. I, pp. 23–5. This work is the source of much of the information in this chapter.
3 Ibid., pp. 26–7.
4 Transcendental morphology, or philosophical anatomy, has been defined as 'the doctrine that anatomical diversity, as present in the myriad of different species, can be subsumed under one or a few ideal types, which constitute the logic behind the morphological variety, and thus its explanation, transcending the vision of the eye, visible only to the eye of the mind.' From N. A. Rupke, *Richard Owen, Victorian Naturalist* (New Haven, CT, and London, 1994), p. 108. Such ideas were present in some continental scientists' work but were anathema to many British naturalists.

2 Early Days in London: St Bartholomew's Hospital, the Zoological Society and the Royal College of Surgeons

1 R. S. Owen, *The Life of Richard Owen by His Grandson* (London, 1894), vol. I, p. 31.
2 'Description of a Microscopic Entozoan Infecting the Muscles of the Human Body', *Proceedings of the Zoological Society*, III (1835), pp. 23–7; *Transactions of the Zoological Society*, I (1835), pp. 315–24, pl. xli. The modern genus name is *Trichinella*.
3 Owen, *The Life of Richard Owen*, vol. I, p. 49.
4 Ibid., p. 50.
5 Honoré de Balzac, *The Wild Ass's Skin*, trans. Ellen Marriage, ed. George Salisbury (New York, 1901), pp. 21–2.
6 Professor William Buckland was the Canon of Christ Church, Oxford, and later became Dean of Westminster. He was also a noted naturalist and geologist and was the first Reader of Geology and Mineralogy at Oxford.
7 Owen, *The Life of Richard Owen*, vol. I, p. 109.

3 Monsters and Curiosities: Extant, Extinct and Non-Existent

1 'Reading of a Description of a New Genus and Species of Sponge, Proposed Name *Euplectella aspergillum*', *Proceedings of the Zoological Society*, IX (1841), pp. 3–5.

2 R. S. Owen, *The Life of Richard Owen by His Grandson* (London, 1894), vol. I, pp. 128–9.

3 Ibid., vol. II, p. 166.

4 R. Owen, *Memoir on the Dodo (Didus ineptus, Linn.), with an Historical Introduction by the Late John Broderip, F.R.S.* (London, 1866). The modern scientific name for the species is *Raphus cucullatus*. Jean-Baptiste Lamarck argued that:

> In every animal which has not passed the limit of its development, a more frequent and continuous use of any organ gradually strengthens, develops and enlarges that organ, and gives it a power proportional to the length of time it has been so used; while the permanent disuse of any organ imperceptibly becomes weak and deteriorates it, and progressively diminishes its functional capacity.

Moreover, these changes were capable of being inherited.

5 This parrot also had an equivalent on the nearby island of Rodrigues in an analogous way to the manner in which Rodrigues solitaire was the equivalent on that island to the dodo.

6 'Description of the Impressions of the Protichnites from the Potsdam Sandstone of Canada', *Quarterly Journal of the Geological Society*, VIII (1852), pp. 214–25.

7 Letter from W. J. Broderip to W. Buckland, 20 January 1843. British Museum Additional Manuscript 38,091, quoted by N. A. Rupke, *Richard Owen, Victorian Naturalist* (New Haven, CT, and London, 1994), pp. 124–8.

8 Owen, *The Life of Richard Owen*, vol. II, p. 4.

9 The species is now regarded as critically endangered.

10 Owen, *The Life of Richard Owen*, vol. II, pp. 131–2.

11 According to the Bank of England website, this is the approximate equivalent of about £54,000 in 2023 (98,000 Australian dollars, or 130,000 U.S. dollars).

12 R. Owen, Hunterian Lecture, 5 April 1842, quoted by Rupke in *Victorian Naturalist*, p. 70.

13 R. Owen, 'On a New Species of the Genus *Lepidosiren* of Fitzinger and Natterer', *Proceedings of the Linnean Society of London*, I (1838), pp. 27–32.

14 B. Regal, 'Richard Owen and the Sea Serpent', *Endeavour*, XXXVI/2 (2012), pp. 65–8.

15 Oarfish (*Regalecus glesne*) – with a length of up to 11 metres (36 ft) – have been described as the largest bony fishes. They usually live at considerable depths of 200–1,000 metres (650–3,280 ft) and have a large number of dorsal spines along their back. This could conceivably account for the 'mane' that is mentioned in some reports.

16 Owen, *The Life of Richard Owen*, vol. II, p. 133.

17 Ibid.

18 One of Owen's first publications, one of the early catalogues of the Hunterian Collection, was titled *Comprehending the Preparation of Monsters and Malformed Parts in Spirit and in a Dried State* (London, 1831).

4 Dr Owen, Dr Mantell and the Dinosaurs

1 C. E. Curwen, ed., *The Journal of Gideon Mantell, Surgeon and Geologist* (Oxford, 1940).

2 G. A. Mantell, 'The Age of Reptiles', *Edinburgh New Philosophical Journal*, XI (1831), pp. 181–5.

3 G. A. Mantell, *The Wonders of Geology* (London, 1838).

4 *Literary Gazette*, 28 August 1842, pp. 556–7.

5 *Literary Gazette*, 13 November 1852, p. 842.

5 Darwin and Owen

1 Kevin Padian, 'The Rehabilitation of Sir Richard Owen', *BioScience*, XLVII/7 (1997), pp. 446–53.

2 Most of the Darwin letters quoted in this book are available in F. Burkhardt et al., ed., *The Correspondence of Charles Darwin*, 29 vols to date (Cambridge, 1985–). Referred to here as *Correspondence*. These letters are also available online at www.darwin-online.org.uk, accessed November 2022.

3 Caroline Owen's diary is frequently quoted in R. S. Owen, *The Life of Richard Owen by His Grandson* (London, 1894).

4 John Gould was 'Darwin's bird man', overseeing the part of *The Zoology of the Voyage of HMS Beagle* that dealt with birds (vol. III). Owen, *The Life of Richard Owen*, vol. I, pp. 188–9.

5 The original of this memo to Emma Darwin is in the Natural History Museum Archive. The text is transcribed at www.darwin-online.org.uk.

6 Living Cirripedia: *Living Cirripedia: A Monograph on the Sub-class Cirripedia, with Figures of all the Species. The Lepadidæ, or Pedunculated Cirripedes,* The Ray Society (London, 1851), vol. I; *Living Cirripedia, The Balanidæ (or Sessile Cirripedes); the Verrucidæ,* The Ray Society (London, 1854), vol. II. Fossil Cirripedia: *Fossil Cirripedia of Great Britain: A Monograph on the Fossil Lepadidae; or, Pedunculated Cirripedes of Great Britain,* Palaeontographical Society (London, 1851), vol. I; *A Monograph on the Fossil Balanidæ and Verrucidæ of Great Britain,* Palaeontographical Society (London, 1854), vol. II.

7 Owen, *The Life of Richard Owen,* vol. I, p. 409.

8 R. Owen, 'Darwin on the Origin of Species', *Edinburgh Review,* III (1860), pp. 487–532.

9 *Correspondence,* vol. VIII, p. 195.

10 *Correspondence,* vol. VIII, p. 270.

11 Darwin mentioned this prophecy in several letters, the earliest in a letter to Hooker dated 3 March 1860 (*Correspondence,* vol. VIII, p. 115), but its source has not yet been traced.

12 C. Darwin, *The Autobiography of Charles Darwin,* ed. Francis Darwin (London, 1892), and also available online at www.darwin-online.org.uk, accessed November 2022.

13 *Correspondence,* vol. VIII, p. 285.

14 Letter from Charles Darwin to J. D. Hooker, 4 August 1872, Darwin Correspondence Project, Letter no. 8449, www.darwinproject.ac.uk, accessed 12 March 2023.

15 Quoted in P. Harrison, '"Science" and "Religion": Constructing the Boundaries', *Journal of Religion,* LXXXVI/1 (2006), pp. 81–106.

16 Canon William Buckland, DD, FRS (1784–1856), of Christ Church, Oxford, and later dean of Westminster, was the president of the Geological Society in 1824–6 and 1839–41.

17 Darwin, *Recollections of My Mind and Character,* available online at http://darwin-online.org.uk., accessed 23 February 2023.

6 Huxley, the Hippocampus and Histrionics

1 R. S. Owen, *The Life of Richard Owen by His Grandson* (London, 1894), vol. II, pp. 273–332.

2 Ibid., vol. I, p. [8].

3   Thomas Huxley to S Macleay, quoted in N. A. Rupke, *Richard Owen,*
    Victorian Naturalist (New Haven, CT, and London, 1994), p. 6.
4   *Athenaeum*, 3 April 1861, p. 498.
5   *The Lancet*, 2 (1862), p. 487.
6   Owen, *The Life of Richard Owen*, vol. II, pp. 312–14.

7 The Evolution of Owen's Evolutionary Ideas

1   The notion of the succession of worlds echoes an idea of the second-
    century theologian Irenaeus. The notion of a former assemblage of
    organisms being rendered extinct by a catastrophe is perhaps more
    redolent of Aristotle. More recent scientific ideas sometimes parallel
    very ancient thought.
2   R. Owen to W. Buckland, 11 January 1842, BM Add. MS 40,499.252,
    quoted in N. A. Rupke, *Richard Owen, Victorian Naturalist* (New Haven,
    CT, and London, 1994), p. 113.
3   R. S. Owen, *The Life of Richard Owen by His Grandson*, vol. I, pp. 143–4.
4   Article by Richard Owen on 'Anatomy' in the *Dictionary of Science,*
    Literature and Art, ed. W. T. Brade and G. W. Cox (London, 1865),
    quoted in Rupke, *Victorian Naturalist*, p. 115.
5   John Ray, *The Wisdom of God Manifested in the Works of the Creation*
    (London, 1691); William Paley, *Natural Theology or Evidences of the*
    Existence and Attributes of the Deity (London, 1802). In the pearly nautilus
    monograph (1832), Owen includes the occasional Paleyian expression, for
    example, 'The tongue of the Nautilus is a beautifully constructed part,'
    on p. 22. In the same work, he is dismissive of the vaguely evolutionary
    ideas of 'the doctrine of M. Geoffroy St Hilaire'. He also argues against
    'the theory of the simple and unbroken series . . . supposed to be the
    natural distribution of the animal kingdom' and also states that the
    differences between the nautilus and other organisms are 'not less adverse
    to a . . . modern doctrine, which seeks to reduce their varied plans of
    composition to a principle of unity.' Typically obscure as Owen's writing
    sometimes is, he seems to be arguing either against the arrangement of
    organisms in a series of increasing complexity or that there is a single
    all-embracing schema. He quotes Baron Cuvier: '[The cephalopods] form
    not the passage to any other group' and 'that they have not resulted from
    the development of other animals, and that their own development has
    produced nothing superior to them' (R. Owen, *Memoir on the Pearly*
    Nautilus ('Nautilus Pompilius', Linn.) (London, 1832), pp. 1–2.

6 Reprinted as R. Owen, *On the Archetype and Homologies of the Vertebrate Skeleton* (London, 1848). The last part of the quotation is drawn from Barclay's *Life and Organisation*, 1822. John Barclay taught Owen in Edinburgh.

7 G. H. Lewes, *The History of Philosophy from Thales to Comte by George Henry Lewes: Ancient Philosophy* (London, 1867), p. 84.

8 'Vertebral Patterns', *Medical Times and Gazette*, I (1863), p. 35.

9 R. Owen, *On the Nature of Limbs* (London, 1849), p. 115.

10 R. Owen, *On Parthenogenesis, or the Successive Production of Procreating Individuals from a Single Ovum* (London, 1849).

11 R. Owen, 'On the Influence of the Advent of a Higher Form of Life in Modifying the Structure of a Lower Form', *Quarterly Journal of the Geological Society of London*, XXXIV (1878), pp. 421–30.

12 Letter from Richard Owen to the Museum Trustee, Spencer Horatio Walpole, on 5 November 1882, in the possession of the Royal College of Surgeons.

8 Museums and Committees

1 R. S. Owen, *The Life of Richard Owen by His Grandson* (London, 1894), vol. I, p. 32. The catalogues are anonymous; they were largely the work of Owen, but the Conservator, William Clift, may have had a hand in some of them.

2 It has been asserted that Everard Home, who had custody of the Hunterian Archive, may have plagiarized from these works and also destroyed some of them to avoid discovery.

3 R. Owen, *On the Extent and Aims of a National Museum of Natural History* (London, 1862).

4 Anthony Carlisle, *The Hunterian Oration, Delivered Before the Royal College of Surgeons on February 21, 1820* (London, 1820), pp. 18–19.

5 *The Lancet*, II (1842–3), p. 170.

6 The differences between the various breeds of domestic pigeons were used as an example of change in animals under domestication in Darwin's *On the Origin of Species.*

7 N. A. Rupke, *Richard Owen, Victorian Naturalist* (New Haven, CT, and London, 1994), p. 44.

8 Quoted ibid., p. 46.

9 Owen, *The Life of Richard Owen*, vol. II, p. 45. At one stage, he also argued that because Britain was the main colonizing nation in the

tropical world (an assertion that was very much open to question), she had an obligation to include in her national museum a display of large, tropical mammals.

10 R. Owen, *Report of the 28th Meeting of the British Association for the Advancement of Science, held in Leeds, September 1858* (London, 1859), pp. xlix–cx. This report reviewing the history of science from classical antiquity onwards is extremely lengthy; it must surely be an expansion of Owen's actual address.

11 Owen, *The Life of Richard Owen*, vol. I, p. 353.

12 Ibid., vol. I, pp. 355–6.

13 Ibid., vol. II, p. 168. The Garrick Club is a London gentleman's club, founded in 1831. It is one of the oldest such clubs in the world and has traditionally had a membership of distinguished literary and theatrical persons.

9 A Cottage in Richmond Park, by Grace and Favour of Her Majesty

1 R. S. Owen, *The Life of Richard Owen by His Grandson* (London, 1894), vol. II, pp. 383–6.

2 Ibid., vol. I, p. 262.

3 Ibid.

4 Ibid., vol. II, p. 98.

5 Ibid., vol. I, pp. 382–4.

6 Ibid., vol. II, pp. 251–2.

7 Ibid., vol. II, pp. 258–9.

8 Ibid., vol. II, p. 266.

9 According to the Bank of England website, this is the approximate equivalent of more than £110,000 in 2023.

10 Owen's Character and Personality

1 John Bowlby, *Charles Darwin: A New Biography* (London, 1990).

2 P. van Helvert and J. van Wyhe, *Darwin: A Companion* (Singapore, 2021).

3 Ioan James, 'Singular Scientists', *Journal of the Royal Society of Medicine*, XCVI/1 (2003), pp. 36–9.

4 PDM Task Force, *Psychodynamic Diagnostic Manual* (Silver Spring, MD, 2006).

5 For example, J. F. Masterson and A. R. Lieberman, *A Therapist's Guide to the Personality Disorders* (Phoenix, AZ, 2004).

6 R. S. Owen, *The Life of Richard Owen by His Grandson* (London, 1894), vol. II, p. 169.

7 Letter dated 27 February 1857, from Sir Roderick Murchison to an unknown person, quoted in N. A. Rupke, *Richard Owen, Victorian Naturalist* (New Haven, CT, and London, 1994), p. 95.

8 Ibid., p. 183.

9 Letter from P. D. Duncan to the secretary of the Royal Society, quoted in N. A. Rupke, *Richard Owen, Victorian Naturalist* (New Haven, CT, and London, 1994), p. 87.

10 R. Owen, 'Darwin on the Origin of Species', *Edinburgh Review*, III (1860), pp. 487–532. Some online archives of this journal are of the U.S. edition, which appears to have been differently paginated.

11 Ibid., pp. 495–6.

12 Ibid., p. 526.

13 Ibid., p. 521.

14 PDM Task Force, *Psychodynamic Diagnostic Manual*, p. 37.

15 Owen, *The Life of Richard Owen*, vol. I, p. [8].

16 Letter in possession of the Royal College of Surgeons, quoted in Rupke, *Victorian Naturalist*, p. 9.

17 Owen, *The Life of Richard Owen*, vol. II, p. 147.

Further Reading

The partial rehabilitation of the reputation of Sir Richard Owen, over the last few decades, from its low point earlier in the twentieth century has resulted in the appearance of a number of papers published in journals on his life and work. A number of these have been referenced in this book. However, accessible and full biographies have been few in number.

John Murray, *The Life of Richard Owen, by His Grandson, the Revd Richard Owen*, M.A., 2 vols (London, 1894) has been reissued as part of the Cambridge Library Collection by Cambridge University Press in 2011. The long Appendix at the end of volume II, in which Thomas Huxley reviews 'Owen's Position in the History of Anatomical Science', is of particular interest.

The definitive work is Nicolaas Rupke, *Richard Owen: Victorian Naturalist* (New Haven, CT, and London, 1994), but see also his modern biography, *Richard Owen: Biology without Darwin* (Chicago, IL, and London, 2007).

There is a substantial overlap between the two volumes written by Nicolaas Rupke; the latter is the shorter work and tends to concentrate slightly more heavily on Owen, the man, while the 1994 publication focuses more on his ideas.

The early correspondence between Charles Darwin and Richard Owen, as well as the correspondence between Darwin and other contemporary naturalists *about* Owen, is included in *The Correspondence of Charles Darwin*, ed. Frederick Burkhardt and Sydney Smith et al. (Cambridge, 1985–).

A detailed biography of Thomas Huxley is Adrian Desmond, *Evolution's High Priest* (London, 1997).

Acknowledgements

I thank my wife Moyra, as well as Bruna Bekle, Alan Cadwallader and Brian Shaw, who read all, or parts, of the manuscript, offering helpful comments from their different points of view.

Photo Acknowledgements

The author and publishers wish to express their thanks to the below sources of illustrative material and/or permission to reproduce it. Some locations of artworks are also given below, in the interest of brevity:

Bibliothèque nationale de France, Paris: p. 90; from William Buckland, *Geology and Mineralogy Considered with Reference to Natural Theology* (London, 1836), photo Boston Public Library: p. 58 (*bottom*); from Charles Darwin, *On the Origin of Species* (London, 1859): p. 71; from Daniel Giraud Elliot, *A Monograph of the Bucerotiae; or, Family of the Hornbills* (London, 1882): p. 44; from Thomas Herbert, *Some Yeares Travels into Divers Parts of Asia and Afrique* (London, 1634): p. 38; from Alexander von Humboldt, *Beobachtungen aus der Zoologie und vergleichenden Anatomie* (Tübingen and Paris, 1806): p. 103; J. Paul Getty Museum, Los Angeles: p. 121; from Othniel Charles Marsh, *The Dinosaurs of North America* (Washington, DC, 1896), photo Ernst Mayr Library, Harvard Museum of Comparative Zoology, Cambridge, MA: p. 58 (*top*); Metropolitan Museum of Art, New York: p. 69; from Thomas Moule, ed., *Great Britain Illustrated* (London, 1830): p. 14; National Library of Medicine, Bethesda, MD: p. 20 (*bottom*); National Portrait Gallery, London: pp. 6, 33, 94; from Richard Owen, *On the Nature of Limbs* (London, 1849): p. 97; from Richard Owen, *Memoirs on the Extinct Wingless Birds of New Zealand*, vol. II (London, 1879): p. 43; from the Rev. Richard Owen, *The Life of Richard Owen* (London, 1894), photos courtesy of Science History Institute, Philadelphia, PA: pp. 41 (vol. I), 136 (vol. II); from *Popular Science Monthly*, LXXIV (New York, 1909): p. 67; from John Ray, ed., *Francisci Willughbeii . . . Ornithologiæ libri tres* (London, 1676): p. 37; Rijksmuseum, Amsterdam: p. 123; Royal Collection Trust/© His Majesty King Charles III 2023: p. 131; from Thomas H. Shepherd, *Modern Athens* (London, 1829): p. 15; Wellcome Collection, London: pp. 16, 20 (*top*), 21, 22,

25, 30, 56, 63, 70, 77, 80, 110; Wikimedia Commons: p. 45 (photo Michael Fiegle, CC BY-SA 4.0); Yale Peabody Museum of Natural History, New Haven, CT (photo E. A. Lazo-Wasem): p. 29.